FAIR FOODS

The Most Popular and Offbeat Recipes from America's State & County Fairs

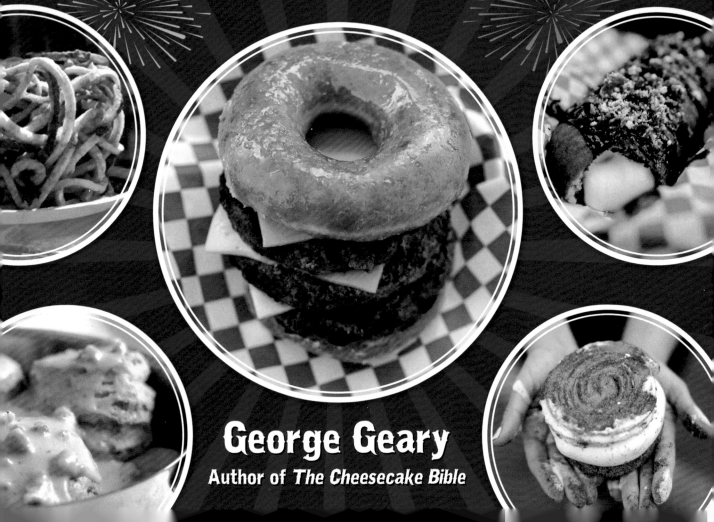

George Geary
Author of *The Cheesecake Bible*

Published by:

Santa Monica Press LLC
P.O. Box 850
Solana Beach, CA 92075
1-800-784-9553
www.santamonicapress.com
books@santamonicapress.com

Printed in Canada

Santa Monica Press books are available at special quantity discounts when purchased in bulk by corporations, organizations, or groups. Please call our Special Sales department at 1-800-784-9553.

This book is intended to provide general information. The publisher, author, distributor, and copyright owner are not engaged in rendering professional advice or services. The publisher, author, distributor, and copyright owner are not liable or responsible to any person or group with respect to any loss, illness, or injury caused or alleged to be caused by the information found in this book.

ISBN-13 978-1-59580-093-0

Library of Congress Cataloging-in-Publication Data

Names: Geary, George, author.
Title: Fair foods : the most popular and offbeat recipes from America's state and county fairs / by George Geary.
Description: Solana Beach, CA : Santa Monica Press, [2017] | Includes bibliographical references.
Identifiers: LCCN 2017020337 (print) | LCCN 2017022636 (ebook) | ISBN 9781595807960 | ISBN 9781595800930
Subjects: LCSH: Cooking, American. | Fairs.--United States. | LCGFT: Cookbooks.
Classification: LCC TX715 (ebook) | LCC TX715 .G31748 2017 (print) | DDC 641.5973--dc23
LC record available at https://lccn.loc.gov/2017020337

Cover and interior design and production by Future Studio

The trademarked brand names that appear in ingredient lists, instructions, photographs, and elsewhere in this book belong to their respective owners and are used here for informational purposes only. The companies which own these trademarks have not participated in, nor do they endorse this book. In no way is this book authorized by, licensed, or associated with the owners of these trademarks, or any of their corporate sponsors or affiliates.

Coca-Cola® is a registered trademark of the Coca-Cola Company
Krispy Kreme® is a registered trademark of the Krispy Kreme Doughnut Corporation
Grape-Nuts® is a registered trademark of Post Foods
Oreos® is a registered trademark of Mondelēz International
Snickers® is a registered trademark of Mars, Inc.
Twinkies® is a registered trademark of Hostess Brands
Jack Daniel's® is a registered trademark of Jack Daniel's
Chambord® is a registered trademark of the Brown-Forman Corporation
Captain Morgan® is a registered trademark of Diageo North America
Kool-Aid® is a registered trademark of Kraft Foods
Jell-O® is a registered trademark of Kraft Foods
Rice Krispies® is a registered trademark of the Kellogg Company

Front cover photos (*clockwise from center*): Triple Cheeseburger Doughnuts (page 93), Deep-Fried Twinkies® (page 66), The World's Gooiest Cinnamon Rolls with Cream Cheese Frosting (page 156), Flaky Buttermilk Biscuits with Italian Sausage Gravy (page 46), and Twisty Curly Fries (page 50).

Back cover photos (*clockwise from top*): Rich and Thick Ice Cream Shake (page 15), Funnel Cake with Berries (page 134), and Caramel Kettle Corn (page 41).

To Neil

Thank you for sharing the past thirty-five years with me.
Here's to thirty-five more.
It has been a carnival ride!

CONTENTS

Fried Everything

The Main Event

Desserts & Treats

INTRODUCTION

If you want a laugh, take someone who isn't American to the fair. Years ago, I brought two British friends of mine to the Los Angeles County Fair to expose them to a little Americana. They were beyond intrigued. They had never seen so many different foods on sticks! In Europe, people do not walk and eat at the same time the way we do here.

County fairs were originally designed for farmers to show off their crops and livestock while their wives competed for the title of best pie-maker in the county. Today—especially in big cities—the livestock shows have moved out of the spotlight, and the food competitions are becoming scarce, too.

For twenty-eight seasons, I was involved in the largest county fair in the country: the Los Angeles County Fair. I started out on a panel of professional judges, assessing everything from cakes and pies to cookies and everything in-between. The competition was fierce! Between judging sessions, I demonstrated recipes in the fair kitchen. Later on, I was promoted to the role of culinary coordinator at the fair. I was in charge of all the competitions, onstage demonstrations, ribbons, prize money, and media. I also had the painful job of consoling the sad losers; every day, I heard that the judges had not given certain dishes their due credit.

In those twenty-eight seasons, I watched as the focus of the fair moved from blue ribbons and homemade pie bake-offs to the rows and rows of vendors that now hawk crazy food combinations from their stands. Around 1980, "classic" fair foods began to evolve from cotton candy and snow cones to bacon-wrapped doughnuts fried in pork belly fat. Not all of the food sold at the fair is fried, but the motto of today's county fair might as well be "Just Fry It!"

This cookbook highlights the new culinary "classics" at America's fairs, from quirky innovations like Fried Coca-Cola® and Spicy Peanut Butter and Jelly Cheeseburgers to longstanding favorites like Old-Fashioned Salted Pretzels, Funnel Cake with Berries, and 1890s Lemonade. You don't have to wait for fair season to make these wacky and wonderful foods—now you can enjoy these recipes all year round!

—George Geary CCP

DRINKS

Spiked Citrus Cooler

This fizzy, citrus-infused drink is quite a thirst quencher.

Serves 2

crushed ice
4 oz. lemon-flavored vodka
1 oz. fresh lime juice
lemon-flavored tonic water
2 lemon slices

1. Fill 2 tall glasses with crushed ice. Divide the vodka and lime juice between the glasses. Top off with tonic water.
2. Garnish with lemon slices and serve.

Misty Berry Hibiscus Drink

A refreshing, colorful blend of berries and hibiscus tea.

Serves 2

crushed ice
½ cup Hibiscus Tea (recipe follows)
½ cup cranberry juice
¼ cup frozen berries
berry-flavored tonic water

SPECIAL SUPPLIES

Cocktail shaker

1. Fill a cocktail shaker with ice. Add Hibiscus Tea, cranberry juice, and frozen berries. Shake to blend and break up the berries.
2. Pour the drink into 2 tall glasses. Top with tonic water and serve.

Hibiscus Tea

2 cups boiling water
2 hibiscus tea bags

1. After bringing water to a boil, turn off heat, add tea bags to seep, and cover for 30 minutes. Cool completely before using.

To make this an adult beverage, replace the cranberry juice with cranberry-flavored vodka.

Blended "South of the Border" Margaritas

Here are two versions of "South of the Border" margaritas: Traditional and Cadillac Blended, which calls for high-end tequila and throws an orange-flavored liqueur into the mix.

Serves 1

Traditional Blended:
8 oz. crushed ice
2 oz. tequila
1 oz. triple sec
½ oz. fresh lime juice
rimming salt

SPECIAL SUPPLIES
Blender

1. Place ice in blender. Fill with tequila, triple sec, and lime. Blend.
2. Serve in a salted margarita glass.

Cadillac Blended:
8 oz. crushed ice
2 oz. gold tequila
1 oz. orange-flavored liqueur
½ oz. fresh lime juice
rimming salt

1. Place ice in blender. Fill with tequila, liqueur, and lime. Blend.
2. Serve in a salted margarita glass.

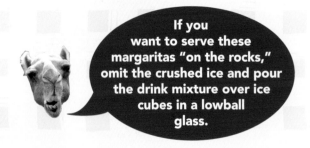

If you want to serve these margaritas "on the rocks," omit the crushed ice and pour the drink mixture over ice cubes in a lowball glass.

Rich and Thick Ice Cream Shake

The perfect classic ice cream shake.

Serves 1

2 large scoops ice cream
2 tsp. chocolate syrup
   (omit if making a vanilla shake)
½ tsp. pure vanilla extract
¾ cup whole milk, cold
whipped cream
toppings (optional)

SPECIAL SUPPLIES
Blender

1. Place ice cream, chocolate syrup, vanilla, and milk in a blender. Blend until creamy, about 30 seconds.
2. Pour into a tall, chilled glass. Add whipped cream and toppings, if desired.

Blanco Sangria

This light and fruity sangria pairs perfectly with the Jumping Cajun Scallop Skewers with Chili Sauce (see page 105).

Serves 8

Two 750-ml bottles Sauvignon Blanc
½ cup brandy
¼ cup orange liqueur
1 medium orange, juiced
½ cup granulated sugar
ice
1 cup sliced strawberries
1 medium orange, thinly sliced
1 medium lemon, thinly sliced
1 medium peach, sliced
One 10-oz. bottle club soda
mint leaves, trimmed (optional)

1. Combine wine, brandy, orange liqueur, orange juice, and sugar in a container. Cover and let sit in the refrigerator for 1 hour.
2. Fill a large pitcher with ice and strawberry, orange, lemon, and peach slices. Add the wine/liqueur mixture and stir. Top with club soda and garnish with mint leaves, if desired.

1890s Lemonade

The secret to perfect lemonade? Tart lemons and superfine sugar.

Makes 2 quarts

2 cups superfine sugar
1 cup warm water
4 cups cold water
2 cups fresh lemon juice
ice cubes
2 medium lemons, cut into thin slices

SPECIAL SUPPLIES

Small saucepan

1. In a small saucepan over medium heat, bring sugar and warm water to a low boil. Set aside and let cool.
2. Pour sugar syrup into a large pitcher. Add cold water and lemon juice and mix.
3. Place ice into a tall glass and pour lemonade over. Garnish with lemon slices.

Egg Cream

Egg creams are popular at state fairs and soda fountains across the country. Ironically, this drink does not contain eggs!

Serves 2

SPECIAL SUPPLIES

Cocktail spoon

¼ cup Vanilla Simple Syrup (recipe follows)
8 oz. whole milk, cold
4 oz. seltzer water, cold

1. In large, tall glasses, add 2 tbsp. Vanilla Simple Syrup per glass. Top with whole milk and then carefully add seltzer water (it will foam and may overflow). Stir with a cocktail spoon and serve.

Vanilla Simple Syrup

Makes 1 ½ cups

1 cup water
1 cup granulated sugar
2 large vanilla beans, split, with the seeds extracted

1. In a medium saucepan, bring water, sugar, and beans to a boil. Turn off the heat and let the syrup steep for 30 minutes. Strain the vanilla pod off of the syrup and cool completely.

Aztec Hot Chocolate

A spicy twist on traditional hot chocolate.

Serves 8

12 oz. semisweet or bittersweet chocolate, chopped
½ cup water at room temperature
6 tbsp. hot water
6 cups hot whole milk
1 tsp. ground cinnamon
sugar to taste
whipped cream (optional)

SPECIAL SUPPLIES
Double boiler

1. Fill the bottom half of a double boiler with warm water. Bring to a low boil. In the top part of the double boiler, combine chocolate and ½ cup of water, stirring occasionally, until melted and smooth.
2. Remove the top double boiler pan and whisk in 6 tablespoons hot water. Pour the liquid into a pitcher or divide among 8 mugs. Stir ¾ cup hot milk into each mug. Add cinnamon, sugar, and whipped cream to taste.

Tri-Berry Spiked Shakes

Made with fresh berries, these colorful shakes make delicious treats on hot days.

Serves 4

2 pints fresh mixed berries (blueberries, blackberries, and raspberries)
2 scoops vanilla ice cream
¼ cup granulated sugar
2 tbsp. Chambord® liqueur
ice

SPECIAL SUPPLIES

Blender

1. Place berries, ice cream, sugar, and liqueur in a blender. Fill the remainder with the ice and blend until smooth.
2. Serve cold in tall glasses.

For a healthier alternative, use frozen yogurt instead of ice cream.

Kickapoo Fruit Punch

This delicious recipe makes a big batch of tropical punch that will knock your socks off!

Serves 8

6 oz. frozen orange juice
   concentrate
6 oz. frozen pineapple juice
   concentrate
1 ½ cups dark rum
⅓ cup banana liqueur
¼ cup maple syrup
1 dash grenadine syrup
1 medium orange, sliced into rounds
1 medium lime, sliced into rounds
1 medium lemon, sliced into rounds
lemon-lime soda

1. In a large punch bowl or pitcher,
   prepare the orange and pineapple
   juice according to package
   directions. Stir in the rum,
   banana liqueur, maple syrup, and
   grenadine. Float slices of orange,
   lime, and lemon on top.
   Top off with lemon-lime soda.
2. Serve in punch mugs.

Mint Juleps

Traditionally served at the Kentucky Derby, mint juleps are sold on hot days at many Southern fairs.

Serves 2

crushed ice
2 tbsp. Mint Syrup (recipe follows)
4 oz. Kentucky bourbon
2 mint sprigs

1. Fill 2 julep cups or glasses with crushed ice, then add 1 tbsp. Mint Syrup and ½ oz. bourbon to each glass. Stir rapidly with a spoon.
2. Garnish with a fresh mint sprig and serve.

Mint Syrup

Makes enough for 34 Mint Juleps

2 cups granulated sugar
2 cups water
1 bunch fresh mint leaves

1. Dissolve sugar and water in a medium saucepan over medium heat. Bring to a boil and remove from heat.
2. Crush the mint leaves and add to the saucepan. Cover and let the mixture sit until it cools down and the mint infuses the sugar mixture.
3. Strain and refrigerate until needed. Keeps for up to 3 months.

Witches' Brew

As autumn nights start to get brisk, this drink fits the bill for warming up the cooler evenings at the fair.

Serves 12

24 oz. apple cider
6 oz. fresh orange juice
2 large oranges, sliced thin
1 tbsp. ground cinnamon
½ tsp. ground nutmeg
1 cup Captain Morgan® Rum (optional)
2 whole cinnamon sticks, broken into pieces

SPECIAL SUPPLIES
Slow cooker or large saucepan

1. In a large saucepan or slow cooker, heat apple cider, orange juice, oranges, cinnamon, and nutmeg until very warm but not boiling. Add rum.
2. Serve in mugs with cinnamon stick pieces.

Chocolate Mocha Shake

A rich, chocolatey shake for adults that packs a punch!

Serves 2

9 oz. chocolate ice cream
3 tsp. chocolate powdered drink mix
¾ to 1 cup whole milk
3 oz. coffee-flavored liqueur
whipped cream
chocolate beans or chocolate curls

SPECIAL SUPPLIES
Blender

1. Place ice cream, chocolate powdered drink, milk, and coffee-flavored liqueur in a blender. Blend until until creamy, about 30 seconds.
2. Pour into a chilled, tall glass. Top with whipped cream and chocolate beans or chocolate curls.

For a lowfat version of this shake, or for those who are lactose-intolerant, replace the chocolate ice cream with "rice cream" and use lowfat or rice milk instead of whole milk.

Apple Slush Freeze

This flavorful, sugar-free drink contain a fresh, whole apple.

Serves 2

1 medium tart apple, peeled, cored, and quartered
½ cup unsweetened apple juice
crushed ice

SPECIAL SUPPLIES
Blender

1. Blend apple pieces and juice in a blender until smooth. Add ice to fill the blender to the top. Blend well.
2. Serve in a tall glass.

To make an adult version of this drink, replace 3 oz. of the apple juice with applejack liqueur.

Pippin and Jonathan apples are fantastic choices for this recipe.

Red Sangria Punch

This rich and flavorful punch is popular at fairs in the Southwest.

Serves 8

ice cubes
4 cups dry red table wine (such as Merlot)
⅔ cup fresh orange juice
¼ cup fresh lime juice
½ cup superfine sugar
2 small limes, sliced
1 medium apple, sliced

1. Fill a large jug with ice cubes. Add wine and orange and lime juice and stir. Add sugar and stir until dissolved. Let set for 10 minutes.
2. Pour the punch into tumblers and float the lime and apple slices on top.

Summertime Adult Lemonade

*Although this beverage is served at many fairs under the name "lemonade,"
not a single lemon is harmed in making this drink.*

Serves 2

crushed ice
2 oz. Jack Daniel's® Tennessee Whiskey
2 oz. orange-flavored liqueur
2 oz. sweet-and-sour mix
6 oz. lemon-lime soda
1 medium orange, sliced

1. Fill 2 tall glasses with ice. Top with whiskey, liqueur, and sweet-and-sour
   mix. Stir and top with lemon-lime soda.
2. Garnish with orange slices and serve.

Watermelon Rum Punch

Watermelon is not just for eating. Paired with rum and a hint of mint, this watermelon punch is deliciously refreshing.

Serves 2

½ cup water
½ cup granulated sugar
¼ medium watermelon, seeded, blended, and strained for juice
4 oz. clear rum
crushed ice
mint leaves

SPECIAL SUPPLIES

**Blender
Saucepan**

1. Bring water and sugar to a boil in a saucepan. Set aside and let cool completely.
2. In a pitcher, combine syrup, watermelon juice, and rum.
3. Fill 2 tall glasses with ice. Pour punch over ice and garnish with mint.

Violet Soda

This turn-of-the-century beverage takes a little work, but it's well worth it.

Serves 1

crushed ice
3 tbsp. Violet Syrup (recipe follows)
club soda

1. Fill a tall glass with ice and add Violet Syrup. Top off with club soda and serve.

Violet Syrup

Makes 2 cups

1 cup water
2 cups violet blossoms (pesticide-free)
½ cup granulated sugar

1. Bring water to a boil in a saucepan over medium heat. Remove from heat and add violet blossoms, ensuring that they are all submerged in the hot water. Cover and let set for 24 hours to steep.
2. Drain off the blossoms. Add sugar to the water and bring to a boil.
3. Cool before using. Keeps for up to 3 months in the refrigerator.

SPECIAL SUPPLIES

Medium saucepan

Lemon Drop Spritzers

This tart lemon beverage is refreshing in the hot summer months.

Serves 4

2 cups crushed ice
6 oz. lemon-flavored vodka
2 cups. sparkling lemonade
2 medium lemons, sliced

1. Fill tall glasses with crushed ice. Pour 1 ½ oz. lemon vodka over ice in each glass. Top with sparkling lemonade.
2. Garnish with lemon slices and serve.

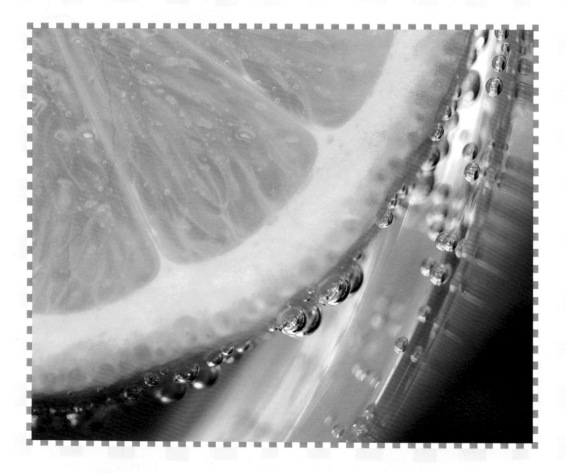

Blended Cuban Mojitos

A minty rum drink that will cool you down and warm you up at the same time!

Serves 2

16 small mint leaves, trimmed
½ tsp. superfine sugar
4 oz. clear rum
1 ½ oz. fresh lime juice
2 oz. club soda
crushed ice
rimming sugar (optional)

SPECIAL SUPPLIES
Blender
Muddler

1. Add rimming sugar (if desired) to 2 highball glasses, and place 7 mint leaves and ¼ tsp. sugar in each glass. Muddle together to break up the mint and incorporate the sugar. Set aside.
2. Add rum, lime juice, and club soda to a blender and fill with ice. The drink may foam up, so hold the top down well. Blend well.
3. Pour into the prepared glasses, and top with mint leaves.

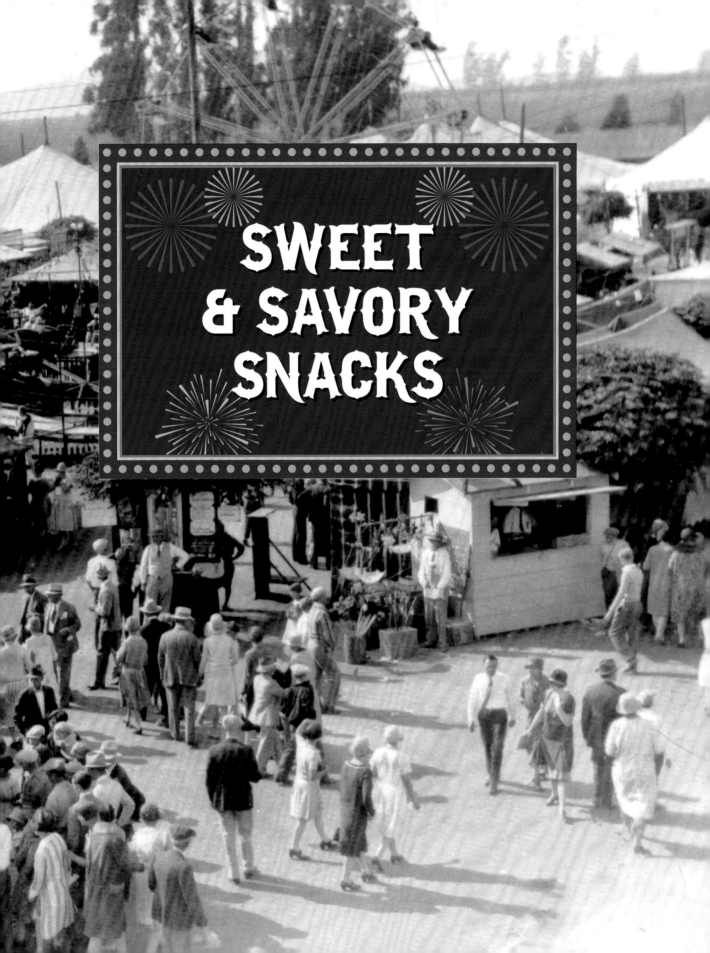

SWEET & SAVORY SNACKS

Bacon-Wrapped Tater Tots with Buttermilk Dill Sauce

Two breakfast foods in one! Paired with smoky bacon and fresh dill, these tots burst with flavor.

Serves 6

1 lb. applewood bacon
2 cups tater tots, frozen

1. Preheat oven to 400°F.
2. Cut bacon into 2-inch pieces. Wrap each tater tot with a piece of bacon, securing with a small skewer.
3. Place tater tots about 2 inches apart on a prepared baking sheet.
4. Bake until bacon is crispy, about 10 minutes, turning over once to make sure both sides cook.
5. Serve with Buttermilk Dill Sauce (recipe follows).

SPECIAL SUPPLIES

**Small skewers
Baking sheet
Parchment paper**

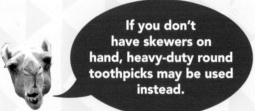

If you don't have skewers on hand, heavy-duty round toothpicks may be used instead.

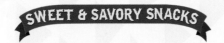
Buttermilk Dill Sauce

Makes ½ a cup

2 oz. cream cheese, softened
2 oz. cottage cheese (small curd)
¼ cup sour cream
2 tbsp. mayonnaise
2 tbsp. buttermilk
1 tsp. fresh lemon juice
1 tsp. fresh dill
⅛ tsp. garlic powder
1 tsp. dried onion flakes

1. Place the cream cheese, cottage cheese, sour cream, mayonnaise, buttermilk, and lemon juice in a food processor fitted with a metal blade. Pulse to blend well. Add the dill, garlic powder, and onion flakes and mix until well-blended.
2. Let the dressing set for a few hours to allow the flavors to develop.
3. Dressing will keep for up to 2 weeks in the refrigerator.

All-American French Fries

At the fair, French fry vendors often offer toppings and dressings galore. Don't be afraid to experiment—try mayonnaise or even vinegar to flavor your fries!

Serves 8

5 lbs. russet potatoes, washed and peeled
ice water
peanut oil
sea salt

SPECIAL SUPPLIES
Stockpot
Candy/deep fry thermometer
Baking sheet
Paper towels

1. The day before making your fries, wash and peel the potatoes and cut into sticks about 2 ½ inches long and ¼ inch thick. Place in a large bowl of ice water. Cover and refrigerate for 8 hours.
2. Pour about 2 inches of peanut oil into a large stockpot and heat to 400°F.
3. Drain potato sticks and lay out on baking sheets lined with paper towels to dry. Fry the potatoes in batches, keeping the oil at 400°F. Turn the potatoes in the oil until lightly browned, about 4 minutes total.
4. Drain on fresh paper towels. Sprinkle with sea salt while warm.

All-American Potato Salad

This savory potato salad pairs well with the Baby Back Ribs with Memphis Dry Rub (see page 98) and the Kansas City Barbecue Pork Ribs (page 106).

Serves 8

2 lbs. white fingerling potatoes, cooked and cut into bite-size pieces
6 oz. applewood bacon, cut into small pieces
4 hard-boiled eggs
1 cup mayonnaise
1 cup diced celery
2 tbsp. Dijon mustard
1 tbsp. Italian flat-leaf parsley, minced
sea salt
freshly ground white pepper

SPECIAL SUPPLIES
Sauté pan
Stockpot

1. Fill a stockpot with salted water and bring to a boil. Add potatoes and cook until fork-tender. Drain and let cool slightly. Peel potatoes, then allow to cool completely.
2. Place eggs in a single layer on the bottom of a saucepan and cover with 1 inch of cold water. Bring to a boil over high heat. Remove from heat and, without draining the water, cover and let stand for 10 minutes. With a slotted spoon, carefully move the eggs to a large bowl filled with ice water. Let cool completely for 5 minutes. Remove eggshells under cool running water.
3. In a sauté pan over medium heat, cook bacon until crispy, about 8 minutes. Drain on paper towels. Set aside.
4. In a large bowl, mash together hard-boiled eggs, mayonnaise, celery, mustard, and parsley. Add potatoes and bacon and blend together.
5. Season with salt and pepper and serve.

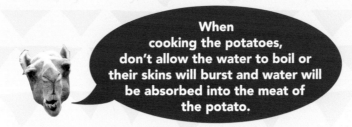

When cooking the potatoes, don't allow the water to boil or their skins will burst and water will be absorbed into the meat of the potato.

Apple Spice Muffins

These muffins have all the flavor of a piece of apple pie packed into just a few bites.

Makes 12 muffins

2 large eggs
¾ cup whole milk
1 tsp. pure vanilla extract
2 ½ cups cake flour
2 ½ tsp. baking powder
1 cup granulated sugar
½ cup vegetable shortening
½ tsp. salt
1 ½ cups apples, chopped fine
2 tsp. ground cinnamon
1 tsp. ground nutmeg

SPECIAL SUPPLIES

Muffin pan (12-cup)
Electric mixer
Paper muffin liners
Wire rack

1. Preheat oven to 375°F.
2. Whisk eggs, milk, and vanilla together in a small bowl. Set aside.
3. Whisk cake flour and baking powder together in a medium bowl. Set aside.
4. Using a mixer fitted with a paddle attachment, cream sugar, shortening, and salt on medium speed for 2 minutes. Add egg mixture and blend on low speed for 2 minutes.
5. Add dry ingredients and combine until only slightly mixed, about 2 minutes.
6. Slowly fold in apples, cinnamon, and nutmeg by hand.
7. Scoop batter into prepared muffin pan, about ¾ full. Bake in preheated oven until a toothpick comes out clean after inserting it into the center of the muffin, about 15 to 18 minutes. Let cool in pan for 10 minutes on a wire rack.
8. Transfer muffins to rack to cool completely.

Deviled Eggs

Many of the barbecue joints at Southern fairgrounds will pop a deviled egg on the plate to add color.

Makes 24 eggs

12 large hard-boiled eggs
⅓ cup mayonnaise
2 strips applewood bacon, cooked crisp and chopped
4 stalks green onion, diced
⅓ cup sriracha sauce
1 small dill pickle, chopped
1 pinch curry powder
1 pinch salt
paprika

1. Cut eggs in half and scoop out the cooked yolks. Place yolks in a large bowl with mayonnaise, bacon, green onion, sriracha sauce, chopped pickle, curry powder, and salt. Blend until well-incorporated.
2. Fill egg cavities with yolk mixture. Garnish with paprika and green onions.

Blueberry Almond Muffins

The almonds in these muffins enhance their blueberry flavor and make for a delicious baked treat.

Makes 12 muffins

2 large eggs
¾ cup whole milk
1 tsp. pure vanilla extract
½ tsp. pure almond extract
2 ½ cups cake flour
2 ½ tsp. baking powder
1 cup granulated sugar
½ cup unsalted butter, cut into small pieces
½ tsp. salt
1 cup blueberries, fresh or frozen
½ cup almonds, chopped and toasted

SPECIAL SUPPLIES

Muffin pan (12-cup)
Electric mixer
Paper muffin liners
Wire rack

1. Preheat oven to 375°F.
2. In a medium bowl, whisk together eggs, milk, and vanilla and almond extracts. Set aside.
3. In another bowl, whisk together cake flour and baking powder. Set aside.
4. Using a mixer fitted with a paddle attachment, cream sugar, butter, and salt on medium speed for about 2 minutes. Add egg mixture and mix on low speed for 2 minutes.
5. Mix the dry ingredients into the remainder of the other ingredients and mix for 2 minutes, until just slightly mixed. Slowly fold blueberries and toasted almonds into the batter by hand.
6. Scoop batter into prepared muffin pan, about ¾ full. Bake in preheated oven, until a toothpick inserted in the center of each muffin comes out clean, about 15 to 18 minutes. Let cool in pan for 10 minutes on a wire rack.
7. Transfer muffins to rack to cool completely.

Caramel Kettle Corn

Fair-goers have been snacking on this rich, tasty caramel treat for years.

3 qt. popped corn, unsalted (or ½ cup un-popped corn)
1 cup almonds, chopped
½ cup pecans, chopped
½ cup unsalted butter, room temperature
1 cup brown sugar, packed
¼ cup honey
1 tsp. pure vanilla extract

SPECIAL SUPPLIES

Baking sheets (2)
Parchment paper
Heavy saucepan

1. Preheat oven to 250°F.
2. If using un-popped corn, prepare popcorn according to the directions.
3. Divide the popcorn between 2 baking pans sprayed with non-stick cooking spray and lined with parchment paper. Sprinkle the almonds and pecans evenly on top of the popcorn. Set aside.
4. Melt butter, brown sugar, and honey in a heavy saucepan over medium heat. Begin stirring when the mixture starts to bubble. Continue to stir for 5 minutes exactly, then remove from heat.
5. Carefully add the vanilla to the saucepan and stir. Pour the mixture over the popcorn and nuts. Stir to combine, then place the baking pans in the oven. Bake for 1 hour, stirring the popcorn mixture every 15 minutes.
6. Transfer the kettle corn to parchment paper and let cool.

FAIR FOODS

Fried Sweet Potato Sticks

One special little ingredient in this recipe—nutmeg—really draws out the flavor of the sweet potatoes.

Serves 8

5 lbs. sweet potatoes
water
peanut oil
canola oil
sea salt
¼ tsp. nutmeg
garlic salt

SPECIAL SUPPLIES

**Stockpot
Candy/deep fry
thermometer
Baking sheet
Paper
towels**

1. A day prior, peel sweet potatoes and cut into sticks about 2 ½ inches long and ¼ inch thick. Place in a large bowl of ice water. Cover and refrigerate for 8 hours.
2. Pour 1 inch canola oil and 1 inch peanut oil into a large stockpot. Heat oil to 400°F.
3. Meanwhile, drain the potatoes and lay on baking sheets lined with paper towels. Fry in batches, keeping the oil at 400°F. Cook, turning the potatoes, until lightly browned, about 4 minutes total.
4. Drain on fresh paper towels. While still warm, sprinkle with sea salt, nutmeg, and garlic salt to taste.

Lemon Blueberry Scones

These delicious scones have just a hint of citrus.

Makes 18 scones

2 cups all-purpose flour
1 ¼ cups cake flour
3 ¾ tsp. baking powder
3 tsp. granulated sugar
1 tsp. salt
1 tsp. lemon zest
6 tbsp. vegetable shortening, cold
¾ cup whole milk
1 tbsp. fresh lemon juice
2 large eggs, slightly beaten
½ cup fresh blueberries
coarse sugar

SPECIAL SUPPLIES

**Baking sheet
Parchment
paper
Pizza cutter**

1. Preheat oven to 450°F.
2. In a large bowl, whisk together flours, baking powder, sugar, salt, and lemon zest. Set aside.
3. In small pieces, add vegetable shortening to the flour mixture. Blend with a pastry blender or 2 large forks until the mixture looks like fine breadcrumbs. Do not over-mix.
4. Stir in milk, lemon juice, and about ¾ of the beaten egg mixture. Mix only until the dry ingredients are moistened. Add blueberries. Gather dough into a ball and press so it holds together.
5. On a surface dusted with flour, knead the dough lightly about 12 times. On parchment paper, pat the dough into a circle about 12 inches across and ½ inch thick. Using a pizza cutter, cut the dough into 18 triangles. Brush reserved egg on top of the dough and sprinkle with coarse sugar.
6. Place the scones 1 inch apart on a baking sheet lined with parchment paper and bake until golden brown, about 10 to 12 minutes. Serve hot.

Popcorn Balls

These salty-sweet popcorn balls are perfect for kids' parties.

Makes 4 to 6 popcorn balls

3 qt. popped corn, unsalted (or ½ cup un-popped corn)
1 cup granulated sugar
⅓ cup light corn syrup
⅓ cup cold water
1 tsp. white vinegar
1 tsp. sea salt
¼ cup unsalted butter, cut into small pieces
½ tsp. pure vanilla extract
¼ tsp. pure almond extract

SPECIAL SUPPLIES

Medium saucepan
Candy/deep fry thermometer
Baking sheet
Parchment paper

1. If using un-popped corn, prepare popcorn according to directions. Place popcorn in a large oiled bowl and set aside.
2. Add sugar, corn syrup, cold water, vinegar, and salt to a medium saucepan. Place over high heat, stirring for 2 minutes to dissolve sugar. Stop stirring and bring mixture to a boil. Cook until mixture reaches 260°F, about 5 to 7 minutes. Remove from heat and stir in butter, vanilla, and almond extract until smooth.
3. Drizzle mixture over popcorn. Stir until popcorn is coated and cool enough to handle, about 3 minutes.
4. Using oiled hands, tightly press popcorn mixture into 3-inch balls. Place on parchment paper to cool completely, about 15 minutes.

Roasted Garlic Pumpkin Seeds

Most state fairs begin just in time for pumpkin season. Here's a tasty use for those pumpkin seeds.

Serves 12

2 whole bulbs garlic
⅓ cup unsalted butter, melted
⅓ cup olive oil
2 tbsp. parsley, chopped
½ tsp. sea salt
4 cups fresh pumpkin seeds, cleaned and dry

SPECIAL SUPPLIES

Baking sheet
Parchment paper

1. Preheat oven to 350°F.
2. Cut about ⅛ of an inch off the top of the garlic bulbs, exposing the garlic inside but keeping the bulbs intact (do not peel the garlic). Drizzle butter and oil on the bulbs and sprinkle with salt. Wrap in foil and place on baking sheet lined with parchment paper. Bake for 45 minutes. Remove from oven and allow to cool.
3. Squeeze softened garlic out of the bulbs and into a large bowl. Add pumpkin seeds to the bowl and stir to coat the seeds fully. Sprinkle with fresh parsley.
4. Place seeds on a baking sheet lined with parchment paper and bake until the seeds are golden brown, about 15 to 20 minutes.

This recipe works best with seeds fresh from a pumpkin, rather than packaged pumpkin seeds.

Flaky Buttermilk Biscuits with Italian Sausage Gravy

Biscuits and gravy are served at many fairs in the early morning, before the crowds get too heavy.

Serves 6

4 cups all-purpose flour
2 tbsp. baking powder
1 tsp. salt
½ cup shortening, very cold, cut into small pieces
1 ⅔ cups buttermilk, cold

SPECIAL SUPPLIES

Baking sheet
Parchment paper

1. Preheat oven to 450°F.
2. Whisk together flour, baking powder, and salt in a large bowl. Add shortening to the dry mixture. Using 2 forks or a pastry blender, blend until the mixture reaches a cornmeal-like consistency. Do not over-blend or it will become tough and create an inedible biscuit.
3. Pour buttermilk into the flour mixture. Blend together with 2 forks until the dough looks like it is completely moistened, about 2 minutes. It may still be sticky.
4. Using 2 tablespoons, drop dough onto a baking sheet lined with parchment paper, spacing the biscuits about 2 inches apart.
5. Place in the oven and bake until the biscuit tops are golden brown, about 10 to 12 minutes.
6. Serve warm with butter or a nice helping of Italian Sausage Gravy (recipe follows).

Italian Sausage Gravy

Makes 3 cups

11 oz. Italian spicy pork sausage, crumbled, with the casings removed
1/3 cup all-purpose flour
2 2/3 cups whole milk
sea salt
ground pepper

1. In a large skillet over medium heat, cook sausage until done, about 4 to 6 minutes. Stir in flour. While stirring, add milk in a steady stream and cook until mixture comes to a boil and thickens, continuing to stir constantly.
2. Reduce heat to low, simmering for about 2 minutes. Season with salt and pepper.

Grande Beef Nachos

This hearty dish can be put together in just a few minutes.

Serves 6

12 oz. tortilla chips
1 medium onion, minced
14–19 oz. pinto or black beans, drained and rinsed
1 tsp. chili powder
1 tsp. paprika
¾ tsp. salt
¾ tsp. dried onion flakes
¼ tsp. cayenne pepper
¼ tsp. onion powder
1/8 tsp. ground oregano
8 oz. cheddar cheese, shredded
8 oz. Monterey Jack cheese, shredded
8 oz. lean ground beef or turkey
¼ cup sour cream

SPECIAL SUPPLIES
Large skillet
Microwave

1. Place chips in a single layer on a microwave-safe platter. Set aside.
2. In a medium bowl, combine onion, beans, chili powder, paprika, salt, onion flakes, cayenne pepper, onion powder, and oregano. Set aside.
3. In a large skillet over medium heat, cook meat until no longer pink, 10 to 15 minutes. Drain off fat. Add bean mixture and cook, stirring, until hot.
4. Spoon mixture over chips and sprinkle with cheese. Microwave for 20 seconds or until cheese is bubbling. Garnish with sour cream.

To avoid soggy chips, do not place the hot meat mixture over the corn chips until you are ready to microwave.

Grilled Corn on the Cob

The fresh herbs in this recipe enhance the corn's natural sweetness, eliminating the need for butter.

Serves 6

6 large ears of corn
1 small bunch tarragon
1 small bunch thyme
1 small bunch rosemary

SPECIAL SUPPLIES
Grill
Aluminum
foil

1. Peel 1 side of the corn away from the cob without removing it completely, and loosen the remaining husk. Do not remove the silk. Insert branches of the herbs against the kernels and smooth the husk back to its original shape around the herbs and corn.
2. Place the corn directly on the coals of a grill. Cover the grill with a foil tent to trap the heat. Grill for 2 to 3 minutes, then remove from heat and serve.

Twisty Curly Fries

Savory ringlets of fried goodness!

Serves 8

5 lbs. russet potatoes
water
peanut oil
sea salt
paprika
garlic salt

SPECIAL SUPPLIES

**Spiral cutter
Stockpot
Candy/deep fry
thermometer**

1. A day prior, peel potatoes and then use a spiral cutter to create potato spirals. Place spirals in a large bowl of ice water. Cover and refrigerate for 8 hours.
2. Pour about 2 inches of peanut oil into a large stockpot. Heat oil to 400°F.
3. Drain potato spirals and lay them out on baking sheets lined with paper towels to dry. Fry in batches, keeping the oil at 400°F. Turn the potatoes in the oil until light brown, about 4 minutes total.
4. Drain on fresh paper towels. Sprinkle with sea salt, paprika, and garlic salt while still warm.

Old-Fashioned Salted Pretzels

Kids have a great time making these pretzels.

Makes 12 pretzels

Dough:
3 ¾ cups all-purpose flour
1 ½ tsp. sea salt
1 ½ tsp. granulated sugar
4 tsp. instant dry yeast
1 ½ cups warm water (110°F)

Soaking Liquid and Topping:
1 ½ cups water
3 tbsp. baking soda
pretzel salt
¼ cup unsalted butter, melted

SPECIAL SUPPLIES
Electric mixer
Pie plate
Baking sheet
Parchment paper

1. Preheat oven to 475°F.
2. Using a mixer fitted with a paddle attachment, blend flour, salt, sugar, and dry yeast. Mixing on low, add the warm water in a steady stream. Continue to mix and increase the speed as needed to mix and knead the dough. Knead for 5 minutes, until the sides of the bowl are clean.
3. Place dough in an oiled bowl and cover the top of the bowl with plastic wrap. Let sit in a warm, draft-free place for 30 minutes. The dough should double in bulk.
4. Meanwhile, make the soaking liquid: Bring water to a boil (212°F), then mix in the baking soda. Pour into a shallow pie plate and let cool.
5. Cut the dough into 12 equal pieces and let rest for 10 minutes. Roll each piece into a long rope about 18 inches long. Twist to make a pretzel shape, and place ropes on a baking sheet. Taking 3 at a time, dip the pretzels into the water/soda mixture and then flip over, making sure both sides are covered. Place each dipped pretzel onto a baking sheet lined with parchment. Sprinkle pretzel salt on top of each. Let rest uncovered for 10 minutes.
6. Place pretzels in preheated oven for 8 to 10 minutes or until lightly browned. Brush with melted butter while still hot.

Gingerbread Muffins

From the county fairs that last deep into autumn, this recipe features bright holiday spices that will have you yearning for cocoa and a cozy fireplace.

Makes 24 muffins

5 cups all-purpose flour
1 tbsp. ground ginger
2 tsp. ground cinnamon
2 tsp. ground cloves
1 cup unsalted butter, room temperature
1 cup granulated sugar
2 cups dark molasses
4 tsp. baking soda
2 cups boiling water
4 large eggs, beaten

SPECIAL SUPPLIES
Muffin pans
(two 12-cup)
Paper muffin
liners

1. Preheat oven to 350°F.
2. In a large bowl, combine flour, cinnamon, ginger, and cloves. Set aside.
3. In a mixing bowl, beat butter until creamy. Add sugar and molasses and blend well.
4. Combine baking soda and water in a small bowl and then add it to the butter mixture, beating well. Add the flour mixture and beat until the batter is smooth. Beat in the eggs, 1 at a time.
5. Scoop batter into prepared muffin pan, about ¾ full. Bake in preheated oven, until a toothpick inserted in the center of each muffin comes out clean, about 22 to 28 minutes. Serve warm.

Cheese Popcorn

Try mixing this flavorful popcorn with the Caramel Kettle Corn (see page 41) to create sweet and tangy "Chicago Mix" popcorn.

3 qt. popped corn, unsalted (or ½ cup un-popped corn)
4 tbsp. unsalted butter, melted
¾ cup cheddar cheese powder
2 tsp. ground mustard powder

SPECIAL SUPPLIES
Microwave
Large paper grocery bag

1. If using un-popped corn, prepare popcorn according to the directions.
2. Place popcorn in a paper bag. Pour butter over the popcorn, close the bag, and shake vigorously. Sprinkle cheese and mustard powder over the popcorn, then re-close the bag and shake vigorously again.
3. Place the bag of popcorn in the microwave and cook on high for 30 seconds to dry out the popcorn. Allow to cool before eating.

If your microwave is on the small side, divide the popcorn into 2 batches to cook.

Maple and Bacon Doughnuts

Once a fad in the '90s, this sweet and savory snack is now a fair staple.

Makes 12 doughnuts

Doughnuts:
2 cups all-purpose flour
¾ cup granulated sugar
2 tsp. baking powder
1 tsp. sea salt
2 large eggs, beaten
¾ cup heavy cream
1 tbsp. unsalted butter, melted
4 oz. bacon, cooked and crumbled

Maple Glaze:
2 cups confectioners sugar
3 tbsp. pure maple syrup, warmed
2 tbsp. heavy cream
1 tsp. light corn syrup
hot water

SPECIAL SUPPLIES
**Pastry bag
Doughnut pans
(two 6-well)
Wire rack**

1. Preheat oven to 350°F.
2. In a large bowl, whisk together flour, sugar, baking powder, and salt. Set aside.
3. In a medium bowl, whisk together eggs, cream, and butter. Add to flour mixture and blend just until incorporated. Fold about 2 oz. of the bacon into mixture, reserving the remainder for the top of the doughnuts.
4. Place batter in a pastry bag. Squeeze batter into a doughnut pan sprayed with nonstick cooking spray, pressing it into every crevice of the pan, about ⅔ full.

5. Bake doughnuts until they spring back when lightly touched, about 18 to 24 minutes. Let cool in the pan for 10 minutes.
6. Pop doughnuts out of the pan and let cool completely on a cooling rack.
7. Meanwhile, make the glaze: Whisk together sugar, maple syrup, cream, and corn syrup until smooth. Stir in additional water to make a smooth glaze that is thick enough to cling to the doughnuts.
8. Dip doughnuts as soon as the glaze is mixed, before it hardens. Sprinkle with the remaining bacon.

Homemade Potato Chips

There's nothing like fresh, homemade potato chips!

Serves 6

SPECIAL SUPPLIES

Food processor
Stockpot
Candy/deep fry thermometer
Baking sheet
Paper towels

1 ½ lbs. potatoes, peeled
2 cups canola oil
sea salt

1. Slice potatoes in a food processor fitted with a thin slicing blade. Transfer to a large bowl, cover with cold salted water, and soak for 10 minutes. Drain in a colander and rinse thoroughly under cold running water.
2. In a stockpot, heat oil over medium heat to 350°F. Add potatoes in small batches and fry, stirring frequently to keep the slices separated. Turn the slices once to ensure they brown evenly. Fry until golden, about 2 to 3 minutes per side.
3. Using a slotted spoon, transfer chips to a baking sheet lined with paper towels. Sprinkle with sea salt.

Pesto Coleslaw

This slaw's rich basil flavor makes it a new favorite. Perfect as a side dish with ribs or steak.

Serves 6 to 8

½ head white cabbage, shredded
¼ head red cabbage, shredded
3 large carrots, peeled and shredded
1 stalk green onions, chopped fine
½ cup flat parsley, leaves only
½ cup fresh basil leaves
1 cup mayonnaise
½ cup toasted pine nuts
sea salt
freshly ground white pepper

SPECIAL SUPPLIES
Food processor

1. In a large bowl, combine cabbage, carrots, onions, pine nuts, and parsley leaves. Set aside.
2. In a food processor fitted with a metal blade, process mayonnaise and basil until smooth, about 5 seconds. Pour on top of cabbage and toss to coat. Season with salt and pepper and serve.

Baked Corn Chips with Traditional Salsa

You're the only one who will know these corn chips are baked!

Serves 8

1 lb. flour tortillas, cut into triangles
½ tsp. seasoning salt

1. Preheat oven to 400°F.
2. Place chips in a single layer on a baking sheet lined with parchment paper. Sprinkle with seasoning salt.
3. Bake for 10 minutes, then turn over and continue to bake until chips are lightly browned and crispy. Serve with Traditional Salsa (recipe follows).

SPECIAL SUPPLIES
Baking sheet
Parchment paper

Traditional Salsa

This all-purpose salsa is great with chips, grilled meats, or tacos.

Makes 4 cups

1 medium onion, chopped fine
1 lb. Roma tomatoes, seeded and chopped
2 serrano chilies, seeded and chopped
¼ cup cilantro, chopped
2 tbsp. fresh lime juice
2 tsp. granulated sugar
2 tsp. salt

1. Rinse chopped onion in a strainer under warm water for a few minutes. Shake dry.
2. Place onions, tomatoes, chilies, cilantro, lime juice, sugar, and salt in a large bowl and toss. Keeps in the refrigerator for up to 3 days.

Ten-Pound Cheese Buns

These pizza-like cheese buns don't actually weigh ten pounds, but they do hit an impressive two pounds on the scale!

Serves 2 to 4

1 loaf French bread, sliced lengthwise
¾ cup unsalted butter, room temperature
¾ cup cheddar cheese, shredded
2 tbsp. parsley, chopped fine
1 tsp. sea salt
½ tsp. paprika
½ tsp. garlic powder
toppings (sausage, salami, pepperoni, veggies, etc.)

SPECIAL SUPPLIES
Baking sheets (2)
Parchment paper

1. Preheat oven to 400°F.
2. Place bread slices on baking sheets lined with parchment paper. Set aside.
3. In a medium bowl, combine butter, cheese, parsley, salt, paprika, and garlic powder. Mix until well-blended.
4. Spread mixture evenly on top of bread slices. Add desired toppings.
5. Place in preheated oven and bake until the tops of the buns are light brown, about 8 to 14 minutes.

Roasted Sugar Pecans

This sweet snack is served at the fair in paper cones.

Makes 2 cups

2 cups pecan halves
1 large egg white, whisked
½ cup granulated sugar

SPECIAL SUPPLIES

**Baking sheet
Parchment paper**

1. Preheat oven to 400°F.
2. Place pecans, egg white, and sugar in a medium bowl. Stir to coat the pecans completely.
3. Spread out pecans in a single layer on a baking sheet lined with parchment paper. Bake until golden brown, about 10 to 14 minutes, turning the nuts to ensure that they are baking evenly.

Spicy Onion Rings

You haven't lived until you've tried hot, fresh homemade onion rings. The spices in this recipe give them a little kick.

Serves 4 to 6

2 large sweet onions, cut into ½-inch slices
2 ½ cups all-purpose flour
canola oil
½ cup cornstarch
2 tbsp. paprika
1 tsp. cayenne
1 ½ tsp. sea salt
1 ½ cups whole milk
1 cup tonic water
1 large egg
sea salt to taste

SPECIAL SUPPLIES

Stockpot
Candy/deep fry
thermometer
Wire rack

1. Preheat oven to 200°F.
2. Separate the onions into rings and place in a large bowl. Toss with ½ cup of the flour. Arrange the floured rings on a cooling rack and let stand for 15 minutes.
3. Pour about 2 inches of canola oil into a large stockpot and heat to 365°F over medium-high heat.
4. In a large bowl, whisk together the remaining flour, cornstarch, paprika, cayenne, and salt. Whisk in milk, tonic water, and egg.
5. Working in 3 or 4 batches, add onions to the batter and then immediately place in the hot oil. Fry until crisp and golden, turning once, 2 to 3 minutes. Allow the oil to return to 365°F between batches.
6. Season the onion rings with salt. Serve immediately with your condiment of choice, or transfer to a cooling rack and keep warm in the oven until ready to eat.

FRIED EVERYTHING

Fried Avocado Slices with Creamy Ranch Sauce

A crunchy coating encases these creamy avocado slices for a tasty treat.

Serves 4

canola oil
2 large eggs, beaten
1 cup panko breadcrumbs
½ cup all-purpose flour
2 medium avocados, ripe but firm, sliced into
   8 pieces each

SPECIAL SUPPLIES

Deep sauté pan
Candy/deep fry thermometer
Baking sheet
Paper towels

1. Pour 1 ½ inches canola oil into a deep sauté pan. Heat to 350°F.
2. Place beaten eggs in a shallow bowl, panko breadcrumbs in another, and flour in another.
3. Using a fork, dredge each avocado slice through the flour, then dip into the egg, and then roll in the breadcrumbs. Press the breadcrumbs into the avocado slices by hand to make the panko stick.
4. Working with 5 slices at a time, drop avocado into heated oil and cook 3 to
   4 minutes until the slices float and reach a light brown color. Remove from oil and drain on paper towels. Serve with Creamy Ranch Sauce (recipe follows).

Creamy Ranch Sauce

1 cup mayonnaise
¼ cup buttermilk
½ tsp. garlic salt
½ tsp. dried dill
½ tsp. dried chives
½ tsp. dried onion
sea salt
freshly ground black pepper

1. Whisk together mayonnaise, buttermilk, garlic salt, dill, chives, and onion in a medium bowl. Whisk in salt and pepper to taste.
2. Cover and refrigerate for at least 1 hour before serving.

Deep-Fried Twinkies®

The Texas State Fair was the first to offer this sinful treat.

Makes 6 Twinkies®

6 Twinkies®
3 cups all-purpose flour
3 tbsp. granulated sugar
3 tsp. baking powder
1 tsp. baking soda
¾ tsp. sea salt
1 cup buttermilk
½ cup whole milk
3 large eggs
3 tbsp. unsalted butter, melted
canola oil
confectioners sugar

SPECIAL SUPPLIES

Dutch oven
Candy/deep fry thermometer
Skewers (6)
Baking sheet
Parchment paper
Paper towels

1. Skewer each Twinkie® and place on a baking sheet lined with parchment paper. Freeze for 2 hours.
2. Meanwhile, prepare the batter: In a large bowl, whisk together flour, sugar, baking powder, baking soda, and salt. Set aside.
3. In a separate bowl, whisk together buttermilk, whole milk, eggs, and melted butter. Pour into flour mixture and blend just until smooth.
4. In a Dutch oven, heat 2 inches of canola oil over medium heat to 375°F.
5. Working with 2 at a time, dip the Twinkies® into the batter until fully coated. Place in the hot oil, turning after a few seconds until all sides have reached a light brown color, about 4 to 6 minutes.
6. Drain on paper towels, then dust with confectioners sugar.

Fried Zucchini Bites

Fantastic with creamy sauces and dressings!

Serves 8

1 ½ cups all-purpose flour
1 cup light-colored beer
2 tsp. granulated sugar
2 lbs. zucchini, cut into ½-inch rounds
canola

SPECIAL SUPPLIES

Large saucepan
Candy/deep fry thermometer
Paper towels

1. In a large bowl, whisk together flour, beer, and sugar to make a smooth batter. Let stand for 10 minutes.
2. In a large saucepan, heat about 4 inches of oil over medium heat until a candy thermometer registers 360°F.
3. Working with 1 zucchini round at a time, dip the pieces into the batter, coating all sides. Place in hot oil, 4 at a time, and deep-fry for 15 seconds per side. Place on paper towels to drain, then transfer to an ovenproof platter and keep warm in the oven. Make sure the oil returns to 360°F between batches.
4. Serve with ranch dressing or mayonnaise.

Cut zucchini rounds that are roughly the same thickness so they will fry evenly.

For a spicy variation on this recipe, add 1 tsp. red pepper flakes to the batter prior to frying the zucchini.

Deep-Fried Butter

When deep-fried butter made its American debut at the Texas State Fair, nobody thought it would take off the way it did. Today, almost every fair across the country sells a version of deep-fried butter. This recipe's two-step process is well worth the effort!

1 ½ cups unsalted Irish butter, room temperature
½ cup light brown sugar, packed
3 ½ tsp. ground cinnamon
1 cup all-purpose flour
1 tsp. baking powder
¼ tsp. sea salt
1 cup buttermilk
2 large eggs, beaten
2 tbsp. granulated sugar
canola oil
¼ cup confectioners sugar

SPECIAL SUPPLIES

Spring-loaded melon baller
Stockpot
Candy/deep fry thermometer
Skewers
Baking sheet
Paper towels

1. Using a spring-loaded melon baller, scoop butter into round balls and place on baking sheets lined with paper towels. Place in freezer to firm.
2. In a small bowl, combine light brown sugar and 1 ½ tsp. cinnamon. Roll each butter ball in the mixture and place back into freezer. Freeze for 2 hours.
3. In a large bowl, whisk together flour, baking powder, salt, and remaining cinnamon. Set aside.
4. In a medium bowl, whisk together buttermilk, eggs, and sugar. Stir buttermilk mixture into dry mixture. It should have the consistency of thick pancake batter that will adhere to the butter balls. Add additional flour if needed.
5. Pour 1 ½ to 2 inches of canola oil into a stockpot. Heat to 375°F.
6. Take butter balls out of the freezer and insert a skewer into each one. Dip in the batter to coat completely, then drop into the hot oil and cook, turning periodically, until golden brown and puffy, about 2 minutes.
7. Place on paper towels to drain. Dust with confectioners sugar.

Fried Greek Olives

This delicious pop-in-your-mouth snack makes a great party appetizer.

Serves 4 to 6

1 cup Greek olives, pitted
½ cup all-purpose flour
2 tbsp. Parmesan cheese, grated fine
½ cup fine breadcrumbs
1 large egg, beaten well
canola oil
¼ cup mayonnaise

SPECIAL SUPPLIES
Sauté pan
Baking sheet
Paper towels

1. Dry off the olives and set aside.
2. Place flour and Parmesan cheese in a shallow dish and stir to combine. Place breadcrumbs in a separate shallow dish.
3. Place egg in a small bowl.
4. Pour about 1 ½ inches of canola oil into a sauté pan. Heat to 350°F.
5. Dredge olives through flour mixture 1 at a time, then dip them in egg mixture, and then roll them in breadcrumbs. Fry olives in the hot oil until golden brown, 1 to 2 minutes.
6. Drain olives on paper towels and serve hot with mayonnaise.

Fried Banana Chips

Inspired by chifles—Puerto Rican plantain chips— these fried banana chips are mixed with curry powder for a new twist on the traditional flavor.

Serves 8

1 ½ qt. cold water
pinch curry powder
4 large, firm bananas
canola oil

SPECIAL SUPPLIES

Sauté pan
Candy/deep fry thermometer
Baking sheet
Paper towels

1. Whisk water and curry powder together in a large bowl.
2. Slice bananas thin and submerge in water. Let soak for 5 minutes. Remove and pat dry with paper towels. Place on baking sheets lined with paper towels.
3. Pour about 1 ½ inches of canola oil in a sauté pan and heat to 350°. Drop a handful of banana slices into the hot oil and cook, turning slices with a slotted spoon.
4. Once the edges of the bananas stop bubbling, scoop slices out of oil and drain on top of paper towels. Repeat with the remaining banana slices.

For a variation on this recipe, try seasoning the banana slices with salt, pepper, fresh herbs, and spices. Have fun and experiment!

Fried Coca-Cola®

First created for the 2006 Texas State Fair, by the following fair season fried Coca-Cola® was being sold at nearly every state fair.

Serves 4

2 large eggs
1 cup Coca-Cola®
2 tbsp. granulated sugar
1 ½–2 cups all-purpose flour
1 tsp. baking soda
pinch sea salt
pinch ground cinnamon
canola oil
confectioners sugar
whipped cream
maraschino cherries (optional)

SPECIAL SUPPLIES
Stockpot
Candy/deep fry thermometer
Spring-loaded ice cream scoop
Baking sheet
Parchment paper

1. Whisk together eggs, Coca-Cola®, and sugar in a large bowl. Set aside.
2. In another large bowl, whisk together 1 cup of flour, baking soda, salt, and ground cinnamon. Add Coca-Cola® mixture and whisk until smooth. Add additional flour, blending until batter is smooth and very thick.
3. Pour 1 ½ to 2 inches canola oil into a stockpot. Heat to 375°F.
4. Dip a spring-loaded ice cream scoop into warm water and scoop balls of the batter into the hot oil, turning them in the oil until golden brown and puffy, about 3 minutes.
5. Place on paper towels to drain. Dust with confectioners sugar.
6. Serve in a cup with whipped cream and a cherry.

Deep-Fried Snickers® Bars

*Other candy bars may be used for this recipe, but Snickers®
was used for the first fried chocolate bar and is still the best.*

Serves 4

4 large (or 16 fun-size) Snickers® chocolate bars
1 cup cake flour
2 tsp. baking soda
¾ cup tonic water
canola oil

SPECIAL SUPPLIES

Stockpot
**Candy/deep fry
thermometer**
Skewers (16)
Tongs
Baking sheet
**Parchment
paper**

1. If using large chocolate bars,
   cut each bar into 4 equal
   pieces. Skewer through the
   cut side of the bars. Place
   the skewers on baking sheets
   lined with parchment paper
   and place in freezer for 30
   minutes.
2. In a stockpot, heat about
   1 ½ inches of canola oil over
   medium heat to 350°F.
3. Whisk flour and baking soda
   together in a medium bowl.
   Whisk in the tonic water to
   make a smooth batter (it
   should have the consistency
   of pancake batter).
4. Take the skewered chocolate bars out of the freezer and dip each bar into
   the batter, a few at a time. Place the bars into the hot oil and fry until the
   batter reaches a light brown color, about 2 minutes total.
5. Use tongs to remove the bars from the oil and drain on paper towels.
   Continue until all of the candy bars have been cooked. Allow to cool, and
   serve warm.

Fried Mozzarella Sticks

Melted cheese plus a crunchy, savory coating equals pure happiness!

Serves 4

16 oz. mozzarella cheese
⅔ cup all-purpose flour
⅓ cup cornstarch
2 large eggs, beaten
¼ cup cold water
1 ½ cups Italian breadcrumbs
½ tsp. garlic powder
¼ tsp. oregano
canola oil

SPECIAL SUPPLIES
Dutch oven
Candy/deep fry thermometer
Baking sheet
Parchment paper
Paper towels

1. Cut the mozzarella into "sticks" (if purchased in a full ball). Place mozzarella sticks on baking sheets lined with parchment paper. Refrigerate until ready to use.
2. Combine flour and cornstarch in a shallow bowl. Set aside.
3. In a separate shallow bowl, whisk eggs and water together. Set aside.
4. In a third shallow bowl, combine breadcrumbs, garlic powder, and oregano. Set aside.
5. Pour 1 ½ inches of canola oil into a Dutch oven. Heat over medium heat to 365°F.
6. One at a time, coat mozzarella sticks in the flour mixture, then the egg mixture, and then the breadcrumb mixture. Fry until golden brown, about 30 seconds, turning halfway through. Remove from heat and drain on paper towels.
7. Serve with Traditional Salsa (see page 58).

Fried Guacamole Bites

These bites have a nice, crunchy outer layer with a creamy center.

Serves 8

3 medium avocados, ripe yet firm
½ cup red onion, minced
¼ cup shallots, minced
4 stalks green onions, chopped fine
2 tbsp. cilantro, minced
2 tsp. fresh lime juice
1 tsp. fresh lime zest
½ tsp. sea salt
½ tsp. freshly ground pepper
3 large eggs, beaten
3 tbsp. cold water
¾ cup all-purpose flour
2 cups breadcrumbs
canola oil
sea salt

SPECIAL SUPPLIES

Dutch oven
Baking pan
(8 by 8-inch)
Plastic wrap
Candy/deep fry
thermometer
Short skewers
Baking sheet
Parchment
paper

1. Mash avocados with a fork in a bowl. Add red onion, shallots, green onions, cilantro, lime juice, zest, salt, and pepper.
2. Spoon mixture into an 8 by 8-inch baking pan lined with parchment paper, and smooth into an even layer. Cover with plastic wrap and freeze until solid, about 8 hours.
3. About 45 minutes prior to serving, beat eggs with the cold water in a shallow dish. Place flour and breadcrumbs separately in shallow dishes.
4. Take frozen avocado out of the freezer and invert on a cutting board. Cut into 16 squares and insert a small skewer into each.
5. Dip each avocado square in the flour, then the egg mixture, and then the breadcrumbs. Dip once more in the eggs and breadcrumbs. Place on a baking sheet lined with parchment paper and place back into the freezer.

6. Pour 2 inches of oil in a Dutch oven over medium heat. Heat to 350°F. Fry each guacamole square until light brown, then remove with a slotted spoon and drain on paper towels. Fry only a few at a time to keep the oil temperature high.
7. Serve warm with Traditional Salsa (see page 58).

Monte Cristo Squares

These squares are pure fried goodness.

Serves 2

4 slices white bread
¼ cup mayonnaise
4 slices Gouda cheese
4 slices roasted turkey
2 slices honey ham
4 large eggs, beaten
3 tbsp. whole milk
3 tbsp. canola oil
2 tbsp. unsalted butter
   at room temperature
berry jam
confectioners sugar

1. Lay out the 4 pieces of bread. Spread mayonnaise on 2 of the slices and top each with 2 slices of cheese, 2 slices of turkey, and 1 slice of ham. Add the other piece of bread on top, then wrap tightly in plastic wrap. Refrigerate for 20 minutes.
2. Whisk eggs and milk together in a shallow bowl. Set aside.
3. Heat oil and butter in a skillet over high heat. Take sandwiches out of the refrigerator and cut the sandwiches into fourths.
4. Dip each square into egg mixture, then place directly on the hot skillet. Cook on 1 side for about 5 minutes. Turn over and cook the second side until light brown.
5. Serve hot with a spoonful of berry jam and a dusting of confectioners sugar.

Fried Jalapeño Poppers

These spicy poppers pair perfectly with Blended "South of the Border" Margaritas (see page 14).

Makes 15 poppers

8 oz. jalapeños
8 oz. cream cheese at room temperature
1 tbsp. freshly squeezed lime juice
1 tsp. fresh dill, chopped
¼ tsp. garlic powder
¼ tsp. onion powder
¼ tsp. sea salt
1 cup whole milk
1 cup all-purpose flour
1 cup Italian breadcrumbs
canola oil

SPECIAL SUPPLIES

Stockpot
Candy/deep fry thermometer
Melon baller
Rubber gloves
Baking sheets (2)
Parchment paper
Paper towels

1. Wear gloves when handling the jalapeños. Wash and dry peppers, then cut off tops and bottoms. Cut jalapeños into 1-inch rings. Remove seeds and inner ribs. Set on baking sheets lined with parchment paper.
2. Combine cream cheese, lime juice, dill, garlic powder, onion powder, and salt in a bowl. Using a small knife, fill each jalapeño ring with cream cheese mixture, smoothing it out. Return to baking sheets.
3. Place milk, flour, and breadcrumbs separately in shallow bowls. Dip each popper in milk, then roll in flour. Place on prepared baking sheet and let sit for 5 minutes.
4. Dip each popper in milk again and then in the breadcrumbs, making sure to coat the entire popper. Refrigerate for another 5 minutes while you are heating the oil.
5. Pour 2 inches of oil in a stockpot and heat to 350°F. Add poppers to the oil a few at a time, turning them over to get a nice light brown coat, about 5 minutes.
6. Transfer to paper towels and season with salt. Let stand for a few minutes to cool. Serve with Traditional Salsa (see page 58).

Deep-Fried Pepper Rings

These pepper rings make a delicious burger topping.

Serves 6

canola oil
1 cup all-purpose flour
1 tsp. sea salt
½ tsp. freshly ground black pepper
¼ tsp. red pepper flakes
4 large eggs, beaten
2 cups Italian breadcrumbs
4 large bell peppers (red, green, orange, and yellow)

SPECIAL SUPPLIES

Deep
sauté pan
Candy/deep fry
thermometer
Baking sheet
Paper towels

1. In a deep sauté pan, heat about 1 ½ inches of canola oil to 350°F.
2. Cut bell peppers into "rings" and remove seeds and membranes. Place rings on paper towels.
3. In a shallow bowl, blend together flour, salt, pepper, and red pepper flakes. Place beaten eggs in another shallow bowl, and breadcrumbs in a third shallow bowl. Line up the 3 dishes in a row. Dredge the bell pepper rings through the flour with a fork, and then dip into the eggs before dredging them through the breadcrumbs. Press breadcrumbs onto the bell pepper rings by hand to help them stick.
4. Drop rings about 2 at a time into the heated oil. Cook 3 to 4 minutes, until they float and turn a light brown color.
5. Remove rings and let drain on the paper towels. Repeat until all the rings are fried.

Deep-Fried Pizza Logs

Pizza in a log! Fast to pop in your mouth and easy to eat while walking around the fair.

Dough:
1 tbsp. granulated sugar
1 tsp. active dry yeast
1 cup water (115°F)
¼ cup olive oil
3 ¼ cups all-purpose flour
1 tsp. sea salt

Pizza Logs:
1 lb. mozzarella cheese, sliced into wedges
1 lb. pepperoni, sliced
canola oil

SPECIAL SUPPLIES

Food processor
Stockpot
Candy/deep fry thermometer
Paper towels

1. In a small bowl, combine sugar, yeast, and water. Let set for 10 minutes or until it starts to look bubbly. Stir in the olive oil.
2. Add flour and salt to a food processor fitted with a dough blade. With the motor running, pour liquid yeast mixture through the feed tube until the dough starts to collect and form a ball, about 3 minutes.
3. Place in a covered, oiled bowl until doubled, about 60 to 90 minutes.
4. Preheat oven to 425°F. Take prepared dough and cut it into 6 equal pieces. Roll out into a square of about 3 by 3 ½ inches. Wrap pepperoni around cheese, then wrap the dough tightly around the cheese and meat.
5. Pour about 2 inches of canola oil into a stockpot and heat to 375°F. Fry pizza logs in oil until light brown, about 6 minutes.
6. Drain on paper towels and serve hot.

Deep-Fried Oysters with Dill Dipping Sauce

A crunchy coating encases these soft oysters for a delicious contrast.

Serves 6

canola oil
1 cup all-purpose flour
1 tsp. sea salt
½ tsp. freshly ground black pepper
¼ tsp. red pepper flakes
4 large eggs
2 cups panko breadcrumbs
24 oz. oysters, shucked and cleaned (meat only)

SPECIAL SUPPLIES

Deep sauté pan
Candy/deep fry thermometer
Baking sheet
Paper towels

1. Pour about 1 ½ inches of canola oil in a deep sauté pan and heat to 350°F.
2. In a shallow bowl, blend flour, salt, pepper, and red pepper flakes. Set aside.
3. Beat eggs in a second shallow bowl.
4. Place panko breadcrumbs in a third shallow bowl.
5. Line the 3 dishes up in a row. Using a fork, first dredge the oysters through the flour, then dip them into the egg, and then finally the panko. Press the panko onto the oysters by hand to help the breadcrumbs stick.
6. Drop oysters about 5 at a time into heated oil. Cook 3 to 4 minutes until they float and reach a light brown color.
7. Remove oysters and allow to drain on paper towels. Repeat until all the oysters are fried.
8. Serve with Dill Dipping Sauce (recipe follows).

Dill Dipping Sauce

1 cup mayonnaise
¼ cup sour cream
1 tsp. fresh dill
½ tsp. dried chives
½ tsp. dried onion
sea salt
freshly ground black pepper

1. In a medium bowl, whisk together mayonnaise, sour cream, dill, chives, and onion. Cover and refrigerate for at least 1 hour.
2. Whisk, salt and pepper to taste, and serve.

Mock Fried Ice Cream

Technically, fried ice cream is not really fried.
But kids love this crunchy, creamy treat all the same!

Serves 6

1 ½ qt. vanilla bean ice cream
4 cups cornflakes cereal
1 cup Grape-Nuts® cereal
½ cup unsalted butter, room temperature
¼ tsp. ground cinnamon
¼ tsp. ground nutmeg
toppings (optional)

SPECIAL SUPPLIES

Food processor
Large non-stick skillet
Spring-loaded ice cream scoop
Baking sheets (2)
Parchment paper

1. Scoop ice cream onto a baking sheet lined with parchment paper. Place in freezer to firm up for about 2 hours.
2. In a food processor, pulse cornflakes and Grape-Nuts® about 10 times.
3. Melt butter in a large non-stick skillet. Add cereal and cook, stirring until it reaches a light brown color and the aroma of the cereal comes through, about 5 minutes. Remove from heat and let cool completely.
4. Place cooled cereal, cinnamon, and nutmeg in a large bowl. Take ice cream scoops out of the freezer and roll in cereal mixture. Place ice cream balls back onto the baking sheet with fresh parchment paper, and place in freezer.
5. Add toppings, if desired, and serve.

> I recommend using regular ice cream, which won't melt as quickly as lowfat or nonfat ice cream.

Fried Pickles

The hot, crunchy pucker of these fried pickles is like no other flavor you can imagine. Pair with ketchup or mustard.

Serves 4

24 oz. dill pickles, sliced into ¼-inch rounds
1 ½ cups all-purpose flour
2 tsp. seasoned salt
2 tsp. garlic powder
½ tsp. freshly ground black pepper
1 ½ tbsp. hot sauce
¾ cup water
canola oil

SPECIAL SUPPLIES

**Stockpot
Candy/deep fry
thermometer
Paper towels**

1. Drain dill slices on paper towels. Refrigerate until ready to use.
2. In a medium bowl, whisk together flour, seasoned salt, garlic powder, and black pepper. Add hot sauce and water to make a runny paste.
3. In a stockpot, heat 1 ½ inches of canola oil over medium heat to 375°F.
4. Dip pickle rounds into the batter to coat all sides. If the batter is runny and doesn't stick to the pickle, add additional flour. If it is too thick, add hot water.
5. Using a slotted spoon, lower the battered pickles into the hot oil and fry until golden brown, about 30 seconds, turning over halfway through.
6. Remove from heat and drain on paper towels.

Fried Goat Cheese Balls

These are easy to pop in your mouth while walking around the fair. At home, they're delicious served on a bed of greens.

Serves 4

10 oz. goat cheese log, chilled
1 large egg, beaten
1 cup tonic water
¾ cup all-purpose flour
¼ cup cornstarch
sea salt
3 cups Italian breadcrumbs
canola oil

SPECIAL SUPPLIES

Stockpot
Candy/deep fry
thermometer
Baking sheet
Parchment
paper

1. Cut the goat cheese log into 12 equal pieces and roll each into a ball. Place balls on a baking sheet lined with parchment paper and refrigerate for 20 minutes.
2. Whisk egg and tonic water together in a small bowl. Gradually add flour and cornstarch, stirring until well-combined and lump-free. Season with salt.
3. Spread breadcrumbs on the bottom of a shallow dish. Dip balls into the egg mixture, then roll in the breadcrumbs. Place in freezer for 1 minute to firm the coating of breadcrumbs onto the cheese.
4. Pour about 2 inches of oil into a stockpot and place over medium heat until oil reaches 375°F. Fry cheese balls in the oil until light brown. Remove with a slotted spoon and drain on paper towels.
5. Serve warm.

Deep-Fried Bacon

When fair-goers taste deep-fried bacon for the first time, their reaction is priceless. The texture is a novel experience.

Serves 4

1 pound thick applewood bacon
canola oil

SPECIAL SUPPLIES

Stockpot
Candy/deep fry thermometer
Long skewers
Tongs
Paper towels

1. Pour 1 ½ to 2 inches of canola oil into a stockpot. Heat to 375°F.
2. Meanwhile, thread bacon onto skewers.
3. Fry 2 bacon skewers at a time in the hot oil, about 2 minutes on each side, depending on the thickness of the bacon.
4. Drain on paper towels.

Fried Green Beans

You'll find these tasty beans in both street fairs and high-end dining establishments.

Serves 8

4 ½ cups all-purpose flour
2 tsp. salt
2 tsp. garlic powder
½ tsp. freshly ground black pepper
½ tsp. cayenne pepper
½ tsp. garlic salt
2 cups cold water
2 tsp. white vinegar
2 large eggs, beaten
3 tsp. baking powder
canola oil
1 ½ lbs. fresh green beans, trimmed

SPECIAL SUPPLIES

**Stockpot
Candy/deep fry
thermometer
Baking sheet
Paper towels**

1. Blend flour, salt, garlic powder, pepper, and garlic salt in a shallow dish. Set aside.
2. Stir water and vinegar together in a bowl. In a separate bowl, whisk eggs and baking powder together, then add to water mixture.
3. Pour about 2 inches of oil into a stockpot. Heat to 375°F.
4. In batches, dip green beans into egg mixture and then dredge through flour mixture. Dredge through egg mixture again, and then through the flour mixture one last time.
5. Slowly lower green beans into the hot oil with a slotted spoon. Fry for 3 to 4 minutes or until golden brown. Make sure the oil returns to 375°F between batches.
6. Drain on paper towels and serve warm.

Deep-Fried Oreos®

Created by "Chicken Charlie" Boghosian at the Los Angeles County Fair in 2002, these treats have become a fair favorite that you can now find at many state and county fairs nationwide.

Makes 36 Oreos®

36 Double Stuf Oreos®
36 skewers
2 cups all-purpose flour
2 tbsp. granulated sugar
2 tsp. baking powder
¾ tsp. baking soda
½ tsp. sea salt
2 cups buttermilk
⅓ cup whole milk
2 large eggs
2 tbsp. unsalted butter, melted
canola oil
confectioners sugar

SPECIAL SUPPLIES

Stockpot
Candy/deep fry thermometer
Skewers (36)
Baking sheet
Parchment paper
Paper towels

1. Skewer each Oreo® vertically, through the cream filling. Place on baking sheet lined with parchment paper and freeze for 2 hours.
2. Meanwhile, prepare the batter: In a large bowl, whisk together flour, sugar, baking powder, baking soda, and salt. Set aside.
3. In a separate bowl, whisk together buttermilk, whole milk, eggs, and melted butter. Pour into flour mixture and blend just until smooth.
4. Pour 1 ½ inches of canola oil into a stockpot and heat over medium heat until the oil reaches 375°F.
5. Dip each skewered Oreo® into batter until fully coated. Place in hot oil, turning after a few seconds to make sure all sides are light brown, about 4 to 6 minutes.
6. Drain on paper towels and dust with confectioners sugar.

Check the temperature of the oil frequently to maintain the 375°F heat.

Deep-Fried Strawberries

This unexpected snack wraps a crispy shell around a tender, sweet strawberry center.

Makes 16 strawberries

16 long-stemmed strawberries
1 ½ cups cake flour
3 tsp. baking soda
1 cup tonic water
¼ cup lemon-lime soda
canola oil

SPECIAL SUPPLIES
Stockpot
Candy/deep fry thermometer
Baking sheet
Paper towels

1. Place strawberries on a baking sheet lined with parchment paper and refrigerate for 30 minutes.
2. In a stockpot, heat about 1 ½ inches of oil over medium heat to 375°F.
3. Whisk flour and baking soda together in a medium bowl. Whisk in tonic water and soda to make a smooth batter (it should have the consistency of pancake batter).
4. Dip each cold berry into the batter, a few at a time. Place into hot oil and fry until the coating reaches a light brown color, turning if needed, about 2 minutes total.
5. Use tongs to remove the strawberries from the oil and drain on paper towels. Continue until all of the berries are fried.
6. Serve warm.

St. Louis Ravioli

Invented in St. Louis in the 1940s, "toasted ravioli" offers all the deliciousness of traditional ravioli, encased in a crunchy fried coating.

Serves 2 to 4

16 oz. prepared raviolis, uncooked
1 large egg, beaten
¼ cup water
1 ½ cups Italian breadcrumbs
⅓ cup Parmesan cheese, grated fine
canola oil

SPECIAL SUPPLIES
Stockpot
Candy/deep fry thermometer
Pastry brush
Baking sheets (2)
Parchment paper

1. Lay out the prepared ravioli on a baking sheet lined with parchment paper.
2. Whisk egg and water together in a small bowl. Brush ravioli with a thin coating of egg wash.
3. Mix breadcrumbs and cheese together in another small bowl. Sprinkle mixture on top of ravioli.
4. Carefully, cover the ravioli with a baking-sheet-sized piece of parchment paper, then cover with an upside-down baking sheet or a large, flat board or dish. Invert the pan, then peel off the parchment paper the ravioli was sitting on, which should now be on top of the ravioli. Brush the ravioli with egg wash and sprinkle with the crumb and cheese mixture.
5. In a stockpot, heat 2 inches of oil to 375°F. Using a slotted spoon, lower about six pieces of ravioli into the oil at a time, turning to brown both sides, about 4 minutes total.
6. Remove ravioli from oil and serve with a tomato sauce.

THE MAIN EVENT

Coconut Macadamia-Crusted Shrimp with Honey Pepper Sauce

This tasty recipe was inspired by a shrimp dish served at a county fair on the Big Island of Hawaii.

Makes 12 skewers

1 ½ lbs. jumbo shrimp, deveined and dry
¾ cup all-purpose flour
¾ cup coconut milk
½ cup macadamia nuts, crushed
¼ cup unsweetened coconut

SPECIAL SUPPLIES

**Skewers (12)
Baking sheet
Parchment
paper**

1. Preheat oven to 400°F.
2. Thread shrimp on skewers, 3 shrimp per skewer. Place flour and coconut milk separately in shallow bowls. In a third shallow bowl, blend macadamia nuts and coconut.
3. Dredge shrimp through flour, dip in coconut milk, and then dredge through nut-and-coconut mixture.
4. Place shrimp skewers on prepared baking sheet and bake for 10 to 15 minutes or until cooked through. Serve with Honey Pepper Sauce (recipe follows).

Honey Pepper Sauce

Makes 1 cup

1 cup honey
2 tsp. prepared mustard
1 tsp. hot sauce
½ tsp. red pepper flakes

1. In a medium bowl, whisk together honey, mustard, hot sauce, and red pepper flakes.

Triple Cheeseburger Doughnuts

Sandwiching a triple cheeseburger between a glazed doughnut is just a heart attack waiting to happen! This popular creation was first served at the Iowa State Fair.

Makes 2 burgers

1 ½ lbs. ground grass-fed chuck (80% lean)
garlic salt
sea salt
freshly ground black pepper
1 ½ tbsp. canola oil
6 slices American cheese
2 large glazed doughnuts, split in half

SPECIAL SUPPLIES

Grill pan or barbecue

1. Divide the ground meat into 6 equal portions. Form each portion loosely into a ¼-inch-thick burger and make a deep depression in the center of the patties with your thumb. Season both sides of each burger with garlic salt, sea salt, and pepper.
2. In a grill pan on high heat, bring oil to almost shimmering.
3. Cook the burgers until golden brown on the first side, about 3 minutes. Flip and cook for 3 additional minutes for medium rare. Don't press meat down while cooking. Top with cheese.
4. Toast doughnut halves by placing them on a hot grill pan or grill, cut side down.
5. Add any desired condiments to the doughnuts. Sandwich burger patties between doughnut halves and serve.

Freezing the doughnuts ahead of time will make them easier to cut.

Barbecue Turkey Legs with Basting Sauce

You will see these turkey legs sold at both county fairs and Renaissance fairs. Perfect for your little merry maidens and knights of the Round Table.

Makes 4 turkey legs

Brine Solution:
4 qt. cold water
1 cup kosher salt
¼ cup packed brown sugar
2 tbsp. tarragon

Turkey Legs:
4 large turkey legs
¼ cup canola oil
sea salt to taste
freshly ground pepper to taste

Basting Sauce:
¾ cup honey
2 tbsp. packed brown sugar
2 tbsp. tomato paste
1 tbsp. Worcestershire sauce
1 tbsp. red wine vinegar

SPECIAL SUPPLIES
Grill
Paper towels
Aluminum foil

If needed, cut the turkey legs open to check doneness. After brining, the turkey will be fairly resistant to over-cooking and will retain moisture well.

1. Whisk water, salt, brown sugar, and tarragon together in a large container. Submerge turkey legs, weighing them down with a heavy plate if you need to. Let soak for a minimum of 4 hours and no longer than 24 hours.
2. One hour prior to cooking, remove legs and pat dry with paper towels. Rub legs with oil and sprinkle with salt and pepper.
3. Cook legs on a high-heat grill for 15 to 20 minutes.
4. While the legs are cooking, make the sauce: In a bowl, combine honey, brown sugar, tomato paste, Worcestershire sauce, and red wine vinegar. Brush on turkey legs during the last 10 minutes of grilling.
5. When done, transfer legs from the grill to a platter or plate and cover with foil. Allow to rest about 10 to 15 minutes.

If you are cooking over higher direct heat, the turkey legs may cook faster. Be careful not to burn.

Corn Dogs

I created this recipe for the Walt Disney Company back when I was working as their pastry chef. One year, Disneyland hosted a county fair-themed week, featuring a midway, a parade of farm animals, fried foods, and an old vending cart on Main Street that sold these corn dogs. Today, you can still order the same corn dogs from the Big Red Wagon on Main Street.

1 ¼ cups all-purpose flour
1 cup yellow cornmeal
1 tbsp. granulated sugar
1 tsp. baking powder
½ tsp. sea salt
1 ½ tsp. dry mustard powder
12 oz. whole milk
1 large egg
canola oil
1 tbsp. honey

SPECIAL SUPPLIES

Medium saucepan
Candy/deep fry thermometer
Paper towels

1. Whisk flour, cornmeal, sugar, baking powder, salt, and mustard powder together in a large bowl. Set aside.
2. In another bowl, whisk together milk, egg, 2 tbsp. canola oil, and honey. Blend into the dry mixture and set aside.
3. In a saucepan over medium heat, heat canola oil to 375°F.
4. Skewer each hot dog with a bamboo skewer. Dry off the hot dogs with paper towels (the batter won't stick if they are wet), then dip into batter until fully coated. Fry in the saucepan until the corn dogs are light brown on all sides, about 5 to 7 minutes.
5. Let drain on paper towels for a few minutes before serving.

Pickle Dogs

One of the simplest fair foods and, weirdly, one of the healthiest. This is a favorite at the Minnesota State Fair.

Serves 6

6 slices of honey ham
¼ cup spreadable cream cheese
6 medium dill pickle spears, drained and dry

1. Spread a few teaspoons of cream cheese on 1 side of each slice of ham.
2. Place a pickle spear at the edge of each ham slice, with the cream cheese side up. Roll pickle spear up in ham slice. Repeat with the other spears.

Baby Back Ribs with Memphis Dry Rub

A rack of ribs is one of the easiest main dishes to make from the fair. You don't need a grill to make these flavorful ribs.

Serves 2 to 4

1 full rack baby back ribs, cleaned and dry
1 ½ tsp. coarse salt
1 tsp. tellicherry black pepper
1 tsp. orange zest
½ tsp. turmeric
½ tsp. coriander

SPECIAL SUPPLIES
Baking sheet
Aluminum foil

1. Preheat oven to 400°F.
2. In a small bowl, combine coarse salt, tellicherry black pepper, orange zest, turmeric, and coriander.
3. Place ribs on a baking sheet covered with foil. Pat spice mixture onto both sides of the ribs.
4. Cover ribs completely in foil, folding the edges to seal (this will "steam" the ribs as they cook).
5. Bake ribs for 1 hour and 10 minutes. Remove from oven and let sit for 15 minutes before unwrapping. Serve hot.

Firehouse Chili with Peppers

Many state and county fairs hold chili cook-offs, with fire and police departments battling against each other. The flavor of this one-pot chili gets better with time, intensifying after a few days.

Serves 6

SPECIAL SUPPLIES
Stockpot

2 lbs. ground beef (85% lean)
1 medium onion, chopped
1 cup celery, chopped
½ cup green bell pepper, chopped
½ cup red bell pepper, chopped
1 ½ lbs. Roma tomatoes, diced
6 oz. tomato paste
4 whole garlic cloves, minced
2 tsp. chili powder
1 tsp. sea salt
1 tsp. cumin
1 tsp. cayenne pepper
½ tsp. black pepper
32 oz. dark red kidney beans (optional)
¼ cup sour cream (optional)

1. Brown beef in a large stockpot over medium heat. Add onions and cook until opaque. Drain off excess fat.
2. Add celery, bell peppers, Roma tomatoes, tomato paste, garlic, chili powder, salt, cumin, cayenne, and black pepper. Bring to a boil. Reduce heat, cover, and simmer for 1 hour.
3. Add kidney beans and cook for 10 minutes.
4. Serve in soup bowls with a dollop of sour cream, if desired.

Chicken and Waffles with Bacon

In this recipe, bacon is cooked inside the waffles for a delicious balance of sweet and savory flavors.

Serves 4 to 6

1 ½ lbs. applewood bacon
4 cups all-purpose flour
2 tbsp. baking powder
1 tbsp. granulated sugar
½ tsp. sea salt
3 large eggs
3 cups buttermilk
½ cup unsalted butter, melted and cooled slightly
cooking spray
3 cups canola oil
2 tsp. fresh thyme, chopped fine
1 tsp. sweet paprika
¼ tsp. cayenne pepper
2 lbs. skinless, boneless chicken breasts,
   cut into 1 ½-inch-wide strips
sea salt
freshly ground black pepper
2 tbsp. all-purpose flour
1 large egg white
maple syrup

SPECIAL SUPPLIES
Skillet
Paper towels
Candy/deep fry thermometer
Baking sheet
Wire rack

1. In a skillet, cook bacon until crispy. Drain on paper towels and crumble. Reserve the pan and bacon grease.
2. In a large bowl, whisk together the flour, baking powder, sugar, and salt. Set aside.
3. In a separate bowl, whisk together the eggs, buttermilk, and melted butter. Whisk the egg mixture into the flour mixture until smooth. Stir in the bacon.
4. Transfer 2 cups of the batter to a separate large bowl for the chicken. Reserve the remaining batter for the waffles.
5. To make the chicken, preheat the oven to 325°F. Add canola oil to the skillet with the reserved bacon drippings and heat over medium-high heat until a deep-fry thermometer registers 350°F. Add thyme, paprika, and cayenne pepper to the 2 cups of waffle batter. If batter is too thick, add up to 2 tbsp. buttermilk to thin it out. Season chicken with salt and black pepper, then toss with flour. Add chicken to batter and set aside until ready to fry.

6. Set a rack on a baking sheet. Working in batches, remove chicken from batter, letting the excess drip off, then fry until golden brown, 2 minutes per side. Transfer to the rack and season with salt. Transfer to the oven and bake until no longer pink in the middle, about 8 minutes.
7. To cook the waffles, first spray a waffle iron with cooking spray and preheat. Whisk the egg white in a bowl until soft peaks form. Fold into the reserved waffle batter. Ladle ½ to 1 cup batter into the waffle iron for each waffle and cook according to the manufacturer's instructions. Serve with the fried chicken, bacon slices, and maple syrup.

Dipped Roast Beef Sandwiches

A hearty sandwich that is absolutely delicious dipped in mouth-watering beef consommé.

Serves 4

12 oz. beef consommé
6 oz. water
16 oz. deli roast beef, sliced thin
8 slices cheese
4 hoagie rolls, sliced horizontally and toasted
⅛ cup prepared mustard (optional)

SPECIAL SUPPLIES
Small saucepan

1. Preheat oven to 350°F.
2. In a small saucepan, bring beef consommé and water to a low boil and cook for about 8 minutes. Add sliced roast beef. Let cook for 4 minutes.
3. Pile the beef on top of the toasted roll and spread with mustard. Reserve the beef consommé.
4. Place cheese on top of the beef and place in the oven until cheese melts, about 5 minutes.
5. Serve warm with a dish of extra consommé on the side.

For a spicy take on this sandwich, replace the regular mustard with hot mustard.

Beef Teriyaki Skewers

Island flavor on a stick!

Serves 8

½ cup soy sauce
¼ cup canola oil
2 tbsp. molasses
2 tsp. ground ginger
2 tsp. dry mustard
6 cloves minced garlic
1 ½ lbs. cubed beef chuck
8 oz. pineapple chunks
½ cup water
⅓ cup all-purpose flour

SPECIAL SUPPLIES

Skillet (10-inch)

1. In a large bowl, whisk together the soy sauce, oil, molasses, ground ginger, dry mustard, and garlic.
2. Place the beef in a dish and pour the marinade over. Let set for 30 to 45 minutes.
3. Reserving the marinade, drain beef with a slotted spoon and place in an oiled skillet over medium heat. Cook until done.
4. Meanwhile, cook pineapple in the marinade over medium heat until the liquid is bubbling slightly. Mix the water and flour together in a bowl and then stir into the pineapple mixture. Cook until thickened.
5. Pour sauce over the cooked beef and place on a bed of cooked rice.

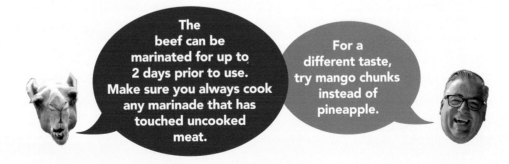

The beef can be marinated for up to 2 days prior to use. Make sure you always cook any marinade that has touched uncooked meat.

For a different taste, try mango chunks instead of pineapple.

Grandmother's N'awlins Fried Chicken

Southern county fairs hold fried chicken competitions, and they take them very seriously. This recipe will have you in the running!

3 lbs. chicken pieces or a whole chicken, cut up
1 tsp. sea salt
¼ tsp. freshly ground black pepper
½ tsp. garlic powder
4 large eggs
⅓ cup water
1 cup sriracha sauce or other hot sauce
2 cups all-purpose flour
3 tsp. baking powder
1 tsp. freshly ground pepper
canola oil

SPECIAL SUPPLIES
Baking sheet
Parchment paper
Dutch oven
Candy/deep fry thermometer
Paper towels

1. Place chicken on a baking sheet lined with parchment paper. Season with sea salt, pepper, and garlic powder. Set aside.
2. Pour about 3 inches of oil into a Dutch oven. Heat oil to 350°F.
3. In a medium bowl, whisk together eggs, water, and sriracha sauce.
4. In a shallow bowl, whisk together flour, baking powder, and pepper.
5. Dip chicken pieces in egg/hot sauce mixture, then dredge through flour mixture.
6. Fry the chicken in the hot oil until brown and crisp. Dark meat will take about 13 to 15 minutes; white meat will take 8 to 10 minutes.
7. Drain on paper towels.

Jumping Cajun Scallop Skewers with Chili Sauce

Spicy and full of flavor, these skewers were inspired by the Louisiana State Fair, where just about everything is Cajun!

Serves 4

¼ cup freshly squeezed lemon juice
3 cloves garlic, minced
2 tsp. Dijon mustard
1 tbsp. fresh tarragon
1 medium-hot chili pepper, minced
1 tsp. salt
¼ cup olive oil
1 lb. sea scallops

SPECIAL SUPPLIES
Sauté pan

1. In a medium bowl, whisk together lemon juice, garlic, mustard, tarragon, chili pepper, and salt. Whisk olive oil into mixture in a steady stream.
2. Place the scallops into the marinade and let sit for 30 minutes.
3. In an oiled sauté pan over medium heat, cook the drained scallops for about 3 minutes on each side. Serve with Chili Sauce (recipe follows).

Chili Sauce

Makes 1 cup

1 cup clover honey
2 tbsp. chili sauce
1 tsp. Dijon mustard
¼ tsp. red pepper flakes

1. Whisk honey, chili sauce, mustard, and pepper flakes together in a bowl. Serve warm or room temperature.

Kansas City Barbecue Pork Ribs

This recipe's special dry rub and homemade barbecue sauce give these ribs a delicious zesty flavor.

Serves 2 to 4

½ tbsp. orange zest
1 ½ tsp. coarse salt
1 tsp. tellicherry black pepper
1 tsp. turmeric
½ tsp. coriander
1 full rack baby back ribs, cleaned and dry

SPECIAL SUPPLIES
Medium saucepan
Baking sheet
Aluminum foil

1. Preheat oven to 400°F.
2. In a small bowl, combine coarse salt, tellicherry black pepper, orange zest, turmeric, and coriander.
3. Place ribs on a sheet of foil. Pat spice mixture on both sides of the ribs.
4. Brush ribs on both sides with with Barbecue Sauce (recipe follows). Cover completely in foil, folding the edges to seal.
5. Place in oven for 1 hour and 10 minutes. Take out of oven and let sit for 15 minutes before unwrapping.
6. Serve hot with Barbecue Sauce.

Sealing the ribs in aluminum foil "steams" the ribs as they cook.

Barbecue Sauce

Makes 1 ½ cups

1 ¼ cups ketchup
1 cup warm water
⅓ cup apple cider vinegar
¼ cup brown sugar, lightly packed
2 tbsp. liquid honey
1 tbsp. dry onion powder
1 tbsp. dry garlic powder
1 tbsp. black pepper
1 tsp. ground allspice
1 tsp. cayenne pepper
½ tsp. freshly ground nutmeg

1. Heat ketchup, water, vinegar, brown sugar, honey, onion powder, garlic powder, black pepper, allspice, cayenne pepper, and nutmeg in a medium saucepan over medium heat. Simmer for 20 minutes or until reduced by half.
2. Remove from heat and allow to cool.

Tequila Shrimp with Honey Mustard Sauce

This delicious grilled shrimp has a little sweetness with a kick of tequila.

Serves 4

¼ cup fresh lemon juice
3 tbsp. tequila
1 tbsp. fresh tarragon, chopped
3 cloves garlic, minced
2 tsp. prepared mustard
1 medium-hot chili pepper, minced
1 tsp. sea salt
¼ cup olive oil
1 lb. jumbo shrimp, deveined and cooked

SPECIAL SUPPLIES

Freezer bag
Grill pan or barbecue

1. In a medium bowl, whisk together lemon juice, tequila, tarragon, garlic, mustard, chili pepper, and salt. Add the oil in a steady stream, whisking vigorously. Add shrimp and stir to coat.
2. Place shrimp in a freezer bag and seal. Let sit in the refrigerator for 20 minutes, then drain marinade.
3. Grill for 3 to 5 minutes on each side. Discard any extra liquid.
4. Serve with Honey Mustard Sauce (recipe follows).

Honey Mustard Sauce

This simple sauce is perfect for seafood. It also makes a great dip for pretzels.

Makes 1 cup

1 cup honey
1 tsp. Dijon mustard
¼ tsp. red pepper flakes

1. In a medium bowl, whisk together honey, mustard, and red pepper flakes. Serve warm or at room temperature.

Grilled All-American Hamburgers

Nothing says America like a juicy hamburger! Use the best beef possible for a terrific burger.

Makes 4 burgers

1 ½ lbs. ground grass-fed chuck (80% lean)
garlic salt
sea salt
freshly ground black pepper
1 ½ tbsp. canola oil
4 slices American cheese (optional)
4 hamburger buns, split in half and toasted

SPECIAL SUPPLIES

Grill pan or barbecue

1. Divide the meat into 4 equal parts. Loosely shape each portion into a ¾-inch-thick burger and make a deep depression in the center of each with your thumb. Season both sides of the burgers with garlic salt, salt, and pepper.
2. In a grill pan or a barbecue over high heat, bring oil to a simmer. Cook burgers for 3 minutes, until golden brown on the first side, then flip and cook for 4 additional minutes on the other side, until medium rare. Top with cheese, if desired.
3. Top the buns with desired condiments. Sandwich burgers between the buns and serve.

Refrain from pressing down on the burger patty while cooking. This presses all of the juices out, resulting in a dry hamburger.

New England Clam Chowder

Fair vendors serve this delicious clam chowder in sourdough bread bowls.

Serves 8

6 oz. bacon, crumbled
1 large onion, diced
3 stalks of celery, diced
1 large leek, white and light green
  part only, washed and sliced thin
2 tbsp. all-purpose flour
4 cups hot water
¼ tsp. white pepper
¼ tsp. salt
4–6 russet potatoes, peeled and diced (about 1 pound)
5 cups whole milk, room temperature
16 oz. can whole clams, drained
⅛ tsp. ground nutmeg

SPECIAL SUPPLIES

Heavy-bottomed stockpot

1. In a heavy-bottomed stockpot over medium heat, cook bacon and onion until bacon is crispy and the onion starts to brown, about 10 minutes. Add celery and leek and cook for 12 minutes.
2. Add flour and stir to coat all the vegetables evenly, creating a golden roux. Add hot water and stir well to avoid lumps. Season with salt and pepper. Cook for 30 minutes.
3. Add potatoes to the stockpot and cook for 15 minutes. Add milk and heat thoroughly, being careful not to scorch or boil the milk. Add clams and cook until heated through, about 5 minutes. Add nutmeg. Season with more salt and pepper to taste.

For a variation on this recipe, try adding 8 oz. of chopped tomatoes and 8 oz. sliced mushrooms to the chowder.

Coney Island Chili Dogs

Contrary to popular belief, Coney Island chili dogs did not originate at the famous amusement park in New York. Two dueling hot dog stands—one in Fort Wayne, Indiana, and the other in Jackson, Michigan—claim to have created the first Coney Island chili dog.

Serves 6

2 tbsp. canola oil
1 lb. ground chuck
1 large onion, chopped
2 cloves garlic, minced
6 oz. tomato paste
1 cup water
1 tbsp. granulated sugar
1 tbsp. ground mustard
1 tbsp. dried onion flakes
2 tsp. chili powder
1 tsp. Worcestershire sauce
1 tsp. sea salt
½ tsp. celery seed
½ tsp. ground cumin
½ tsp. freshly ground black pepper
6 hot dog buns
6 hot dogs, cooked

SPECIAL SUPPLIES

Skillet (10-inch)

1. Heat oil in a large skillet over medium heat. Add ground chuck and cook until browned. Add the onions halfway through, then add garlic, tomato paste, water, sugar, mustard, onion flakes, chili powder, Worcestershire sauce, salt, celery seeds, cumin, and black pepper. Simmer on low heat for 15 minutes.
2. Place cooked hot dogs in toasted buns and spoon the sauce over the dogs.

Belgian Waffles with Raspberry Compote

These rich, fluffy waffles pair beautifully with the tart raspberry compote—no syrup required!

Serves 4 to 6

1 ¾ cups all-purpose flour
2 tbsp. granulated sugar
1 tbsp. baking powder
2 large eggs
1 ¾ cups whole milk
½ cup canola oil
1 tsp. pure vanilla extract

SPECIAL SUPPLIES

Waffle iron
Heavy
saucepan
Mesh
strainer

1. Whisk flour, sugar, and baking powder in a large bowl. Set aside.
2. In a separate bowl, whisk together eggs, milk, oil, and vanilla. Add dry ingredients, stirring just until moistened.
3. Spray pre-heated waffle iron with non-stick cooking spray and cook waffles until brown. Serve with Raspberry Compote (recipe follows).

Raspberry Compote

This sauce also makes a delicious ice cream topping.

Makes 2 cups

3 tbsp. cornstarch
½ cup cold water
3 cups fresh raspberries
½ cup granulated sugar
2 tsp. fresh lemon juice

1. Whisk cornstarch and cold water together in a small bowl. Set aside.
2. In a heavy saucepan, heat berries and sugar over medium heat until they begin to break down and boil, stirring the entire time. Remove from heat.
3. Using a fine mesh strainer, strain seeds from the berry mixture. Return juice to heat and bring to a boil, stirring continuously.
4. Pour cornstarch mixture into the boiling juice and stir to incorporate. Heat until juice has thickened and is ruby red in color and no longer cloudy. Remove from heat.
5. Whisk in lemon juice. Cool completely prior to use.

113

Grilled Pork Chops on a Stick

Pork chops on a stick began to surface at the fair in the early '90s. Watching fairgoers wrangling their giant chops on sticks is entertainment in itself!

Serves 6

1 tsp. paprika
1 tsp. packed brown sugar
½ tsp. onion salt
¼ tsp. garlic powder
¼ tsp. ground ginger
¼ tsp. ground cinnamon
¼ tsp. ground cumin
¼ tsp. dry mustard
¼ tsp. cayenne pepper
¼ tsp. freshly cracked black pepper
6 boneless pork top loin chops, cut into pieces 1 ¼ to 1 ½ inches thick
1 tbsp. teriyaki sauce

SPECIAL SUPPLIES

Wooden chopsticks (6)
Grill pan or barbecue

1. In a small bowl, combine paprika, brown sugar, onion salt, garlic powder, ginger, cinnamon, cumin, mustard, cayenne pepper, and black pepper. Brush chops on both sides with teriyaki sauce. Sprinkle rub over chops, rubbing it into the meat with your fingers.
2. Insert a wooden chopstick into a short side of each chop, about halfway into the chop.
3. Grill on both sides until light brown in color, about 8 minutes on each side.

Buffalo Wings

Buffalo wings are now practically their own food group in the U.S. They got their start in the 1960s, when the Anchor Bar in Buffalo, New York, served chicken wings as an appetizer instead of using them for chicken stock.

Serves 4

½ cup chili sauce
½ cup ketchup
½ cup red wine vinegar
¼ cup hot sauce
½ medium onion, finely chopped
1 tbsp. brown sugar
½ tbsp. Worcestershire sauce
1 clove garlic
¼ tsp. crushed red pepper
¼ tsp. sea salt
¼ tsp. black pepper
¼ tsp. cumin
¼ tsp. cayenne pepper
24 chicken wings
⅓ cup canola oil

SPECIAL SUPPLIES
Grill
Large
saucepan

1. In a large saucepan over medium heat, cook chili sauce, ketchup, red wine vinegar, hot sauce, onion, brown sugar, Worcestershire sauce, garlic, red pepper, sea salt, black pepper, cumin, and cayenne pepper. Bring mixture to a low boil and cook for about 15 minutes.
2. In a large bowl, coat the chicken wings with oil. Grill on medium heat. After about 5 minutes, coat both sides of wings with the sauce. Cook until completely done, a total of 10 to 14 minutes.
3. Serve hot. Use the remaining sauce as a dipping sauce—if you dare!

Mini Barbecue Chicken Pizzas

Tangy barbecue sauce is a special twist on traditional pizza sauce that kids love!

Dough:
1 cup water
1 tbsp. granulated sugar
1 tsp. active dry yeast
1 cup water
¼ cup olive oil
3 ¼ cups all-purpose flour
1 tsp. sea salt
cornmeal

SPECIAL SUPPLIES
Food processor
Baking sheet
Parchment paper

Topping:
½ cup prepared barbecue sauce
12 oz. cooked chicken pieces
12 oz. mushrooms, sliced
16 oz. mozzarella cheese, shredded

1. Preheat oven to 425°F.
2. Heat water to 115°F. Pour into a small bowl and add sugar and yeast, stirring to combine. Let set for 10 minutes or until mixture starts to look bubbly. Stir in olive oil.
3. Add flour and salt to a food processor fitted with a dough blade. With the motor running, pour liquid yeast mixture through the feed tube until the dough starts to collect and form a ball, about 3 minutes.
4. Place dough in a covered, oiled bowl for 60 to 90 minutes, or until it doubles in size. Divide dough into 4 pieces and roll into rounds.
5. Place on a baking sheet that has been lined with parchment paper and sprinkled with cornmeal.
6. Top the pizza rounds with barbecue sauce, chicken, mushrooms, and cheese.
7. Place in preheated oven and bake for about 16 to 20 minutes, or until cheese has melted.

Pulled Pork Sliders

These sliders are a favorite staple at the Iowa State Fair.

Serves 8 to 10

3 tbsp. Hungarian paprika
1 tbsp. sea salt
2 tsp. freshly ground black pepper
1 tsp. garlic powder
½ tsp. cayenne pepper
½ tsp. dried thyme
½ cup honey
½ cup coconut water
¼ cup red wine vinegar
3 tbsp. canola oil
1 medium brown onion, peeled and cut into quarters
3–4 lb. pork shoulder, cut in half
8–12 slider rolls, toasted

SPECIAL SUPPLIES
Slow cooker

1. In a medium mixing bowl, blend together paprika, salt, black pepper, garlic powder, cayenne pepper, and thyme. Add honey, coconut water, vinegar, and oil. Blend to form a paste.

2. Place onion in the bottom of a slow cooker, then place pork shoulder on top. Pour paste mixture on top of pork.

3. Cook pork in the slow cooker on low for 7 to 8 hours, or until meat is tender and easy to shred with a large fork. Cool completely.

4. Pile shredded pork in slider rolls and serve.

Pulled Pork Empanadas

The perfect hand pie—a hot pork and cheese filling enveloped in a flaky crust!

Makes 18 empanadas

Dough:
3 cups all-purpose flour
¼ tsp. salt
6 oz. unsalted butter, chilled and cut into 12 pieces
1 large egg
4–6 tbsp. cold water

SPECIAL SUPPLIES
Food processor
Round cutter
(3-inch)

Pulled Pork and Cheese Filling:
3 tbsp. Hungarian paprika
1 tbsp. sea salt
2 tsp. freshly ground black pepper
1 tsp. garlic powder
½ tsp. cayenne pepper
½ tsp. dried thyme
½ cup honey
½ cup coconut water
¼ cup red wine vinegar
3 tbsp. canola oil
1 medium brown onion, peeled
   and cut into quarters
3–4 lb. pork shoulder, cut in half
3 cups grated mozzarella
½ medium brown onion, diced
¼ tsp. salt
¼ tsp. chili powder

1. Preheat oven to 375°F.
2. Pulse flour and salt in a food processor. With the motor running, add butter, egg, and some of the water through the feed tube until dough forms.
3. Form a ball with the dough, flatten slightly, and chill in the refrigerator for about 30 minutes.
4. Roll out the dough into a thin sheet and cut out 18 round disc shapes. Set aside.
5. In a medium mixing bowl, blend together paprika, salt, black pepper, garlic powder, cayenne pepper, and thyme. Add honey, coconut water, vinegar, and oil. Blend to form a paste.
6. Place onion in the bottom of a slow cooker, then place pork shoulder on top. Pour paste mixture on top of pork.
7. Cook pork in the slow cooker on low for 7 to 8 hours, or until meat is tender and easy to shred with a large fork. Cool completely.
8. To make filling, combine shredded pork, cheese, onion, salt, and pepper in a bowl.
9. To assemble empanadas, place a heaping tablespoon of the filling in the middle of each empanada disc. Fold the discs and seal by pressing the edges of the dough together with your fingers. For best results, refrigerate empanadas for at least 30 minutes before baking.
10. Bake empanadas until golden brown, about 18 to 20 minutes.

If you're having a hard time sealing the edges of the empanadas, brush the inside edges with egg white; it will act as a glue to hold them together. You can also use a fork to help seal the edges.

For a nice golden finish, brush empanadas with an egg wash before baking. Whisk a whole egg or mix an egg yolk with a few drops of water.

Silver Dollar Pancakes

At the fair, these bite-size treats are served on skewers.

Makes 2 dozen pancakes

1 ½ cups all-purpose flour
1 tbsp. baking powder
1 tsp. granulated sugar
½ tsp. baking soda
½ tsp. sea salt
1 ¾ cups buttermilk
4 tbsp. unsalted butter, melted
2 large eggs
maple syrup

SPECIAL SUPPLIES

**Non-stick
skillet (12-inch)
Baking sheet
Parchment paper
Skewers
(optional)**

1. Whisk flour, baking powder, sugar, baking soda, and salt together in a large bowl. Stir in buttermilk, melted butter, and eggs until flour is just moistened.
2. Heat skillet over medium heat until very hot. Drop batter by the tablespoonful onto the hot skillet. Cook pancakes for 2 to 3 minutes on each side. Flip when bubbles start to burst on top of the pancakes, forming little craters in the batter. Cook 1 to 2 minutes longer, until both sides of the pancakes are dry and light brown.
3. Transfer pancakes to a parchment paper-lined baking sheet in the oven to keep warm. Continue until all of the batter has been cooked.
4. Thread pancakes through skewers, if you have them. Serve with warm maple syrup.

Spicy Peanut Butter and Jelly Cheeseburgers

One of the most unusual combinations to emerge from county fairs, this concoction is now served at some Midwestern burger joints.

Makes 4 burgers

1 ⅓ lbs. lean ground beef
kosher salt
freshly ground black pepper
¼ cup creamy peanut butter
4 slices Swiss cheese
¼ cup grape jelly
1 jalapeño, sliced thin
4 hamburger buns, toasted

SPECIAL SUPPLIES

Grill pan or barbecue

1. Gently shape ground beef into four ⅓-pound round patties. Don't handle the beef too much. Press a dimple into the center of each patty. Season well with kosher salt and pepper.
2. Grill burgers over medium-high heat for about 4 to 5 minutes per side for medium burgers. About a minute before the burgers are done, top each patty with 1 tbsp. peanut butter. Top with cheese.
3. Take burgers off the grill and allow to rest for a few minutes. Serve on toasted buns with a dollop of grape jelly and jalapeño slices.

DESSERTS
& TREATS

All-American Apple Pie with Flaky Crust

Nothing is more American than apple pie! Serve this winning recipe with slow-churned vanilla ice cream.

Makes a 9-inch pie

Crust:
3 cups all-purpose flour
2 tsp. granulated sugar
½ tsp. sea salt
1 cup unsalted butter, cold and cut into chunks
½–¾ cup ice water
2 tbsp. unsalted butter
2 tbsp. coarse sugar

Apple Filling:
1 cup granulated sugar
3 tbsp. flour
1 ½ tsp. ground cinnamon
½ tsp. ground nutmeg
¼ tsp. ground allspice
4 cups tart baking apples, peeled and
  evenly sliced

SPECIAL SUPPLIES
Deep pie
pan (9-inch)
Rolling pin
Pastry blending
fork
Plastic wrap

1. Preheat oven to 375°F.
2. Combine flour, sugar, and salt in a large bowl. Using a pastry blending fork or 2 regular forks, mash the cold butter into the flour mixture, blending just enough to create small lumps in the mixture.
3. Using a tablespoon, drizzle ice water over the flour mixture, then blend with the fork until the dough comes together. When you can gather the dough into your hands without it falling apart, form the dough into 2 balls and press into discs. Wrap in plastic wrap and refrigerate until firm, about 20 minutes.
4. Meanwhile, prepare the apple filling: In a large bowl, combine sugar, flour, cinnamon, nutmeg, and allspice. Add apples and stir to coat fully. Set aside.

5. Roll 1 of the chilled dough discs into a circle about 2 inches larger in diameter than the pie tin you are using. Place dough in the bottom of the pie tin and fill with prepared apples, trying not to get any juice on the edges of the dough crust. Top the apples with the second pie crust, then crimp the edges of the dough together. Create an air vent in the top of the pie by making a few knife slits in the top crust.
6. Bake the pie until the top browns and you can see the juices of the apples bubbling through the knife vents, about 1 hour.

Apple Crisp with Pecan Topping

*In the 1980s, the Gingerbread House at the California State Fair sold huge
portions of delicious apple crisp made from tart apples, served with
ice cream and topped with caramel sauce.*

Serves 12

SPECIAL SUPPLIES
**Electric mixer
Baking pan
(9 by 13-inch)**

Apple Filling:
3 ½ lbs. Granny Smith apples, peeled, cored, and sliced
⅔ cup granulated sugar
2 tsp. fresh-squeezed lemon juice
2 tsp. ground cinnamon
1 tsp. pure vanilla extract

Pecan Topping:
½ cup unsalted butter, cold
1 ½ cups packed brown sugar
1 tsp. sea salt
1 tsp. ground cinnamon
1 cup all-purpose flour
⅓ cup pecans, chopped

1. Preheat oven to 325°F.
2. Toss apples, sugar, lemon juice, cinnamon, and vanilla together. Place in a
   buttered baking dish or pan and set aside.
3. Using a mixer fitted with a paddle attachment, blend butter, brown sugar,
   salt, and cinnamon until crumbly. Add flour and pecans and blend until
   well-mixed.
4. Cover the prepared apples with the butter mixture. Bake in preheated
   oven for 1 hour, or until the top of the crisp has reached a light brown
   color and the apple mixture is bubbling.

Cake Pops

These cake pops are simple to make—if you don't take any shortcuts! Follow the directions and your friends will ask you to bring them to every gathering.

Makes 36 cake pops

9 by 13-inch cake, baked and unfrosted
¼ cup prepared icing
8 oz. chocolate candy coating,
  melted and cooled
toppings of your choice (sprinkles,
  chopped nuts, etc.)

SPECIAL SUPPLIES
Spring-loaded melon baller
Sucker sticks (36)
Styrofoam ball (6-inch)
Baking sheet
Parchment paper

1. Crumble the cake in a mixing bowl, add the icing, and mix together loosely. The mixture should form together easily.
2. Using a spring-loaded melon baller, scoop out the mixture and place the scoops on a baking sheet lined with parchment paper. Freeze for 20 minutes.
3. Remove the cake pops from the freezer. Dip a sucker stick about ¼ of an inch into the melted chocolate coating and poke into a cake pop. Repeat until all the sticks are attached to the pops.

4. Poke the cake pop sticks into the Styrofoam ball to hold the pops upright. Refrigerate for 10 minutes to harden.
5. Dip each cake pop into the chocolate coating. Before the coating dries, add toppings, if desired.
6. Poke the cake pops back into the Styrofoam ball and refrigerate for 10 more minutes to allow the coating and toppings to set.

Rice Krispies® Treats

When I was the pastry chef at the Walt Disney Company, we made these treats for a County Fair-themed week at Disneyland. Ours were shaped into "Mouse Ears" and dipped in Belgian chocolate.

Makes 24 treats

3 tbsp. unsalted butter
10 oz. mini marshmallows
6 cups Rice Krispies® cereal
6 oz. chocolate candy coating, melted and cooled
2 tbsp. colored sprinkles

SPECIAL SUPPLIES

Large saucepan
Baking pan
Rolling pin
Cookie cutters (optional)
Parchment paper

1. Melt the butter in a large saucepan. Add the marshmallows and cook over low heat, stirring until melted and blended.
2. Place the cereal in a large bowl and pour the marshmallow mixture on top. Blend with a spoon to coat all of the cereal.
3. Pour the mixture into a baking pan lined with parchment paper, pressing down to even it out. Place another piece of parchment paper on top of the mixture and roll a rolling pin over it to level out the mixture completely. Allow to set for 20 minutes.

4. Invert the mixture onto a cutting board, then cut out individual treats using cookie cutters or a knife.
5. Dip a side of each treat in melted chocolate and sprinkles. Place on parchment paper to set.

Rich Chocolate Fudge

The world's most decadent fudge!

Makes 5 pounds

24 oz. semisweet chocolate, chopped
7 oz. marshmallow cream or fluff
4 ½ cups granulated sugar
12 oz. evaporated milk
2 tbsp. unsalted butter, room temperature
⅛ tsp. sea salt
1 tbsp. pure vanilla extract
8 oz. toasted pecans (optional)

SPECIAL SUPPLIES

Electric mixer
Baking pan
(9 by 13-inch)
Large saucepan
Aluminum foil
Parchment paper
Plastic wrap

1. Line a 9 by 13-inch baking pan with a layer of foil, then place a layer of parchment paper on top of the foil.
2. Place chocolate and marshmallow cream in a mixer fitted with a paddle attachment. Set aside.
3. In a large saucepan, combine sugar, evaporated milk, butter, and salt in a heavy saucepan. Bring to a boil over high heat, stirring constantly. When the mixture comes to a boil, lower the heat to medium. Continue to boil steadily for 6 minutes, stirring constantly to prevent scorching.
4. Pour the boiling syrup over the chocolate and marshmallow cream in the mixing bowl. Mix until the chocolate is melted and well-blended. Beat in the vanilla and add the pecans, if desired.
5. Pour the fudge mixture into the prepared baking pan and smooth to the sides. Allow to cool at room temperature for 24 hours before cutting. Do not refrigerate or the fudge will lose its gloss.
6. After cutting the fudge, wrap each piece in plastic wrap to keep fresh.

Black-and-White Cookies

Cake flour gives this essential New York cookie a light and fluffy texture.

Makes 18 cookies

Cookie:
1 ¾ cups granulated sugar
1 cup unsalted butter, room temperature
4 large eggs
1 ½ cups whole milk
½ tsp. pure vanilla extract
½ tsp. lemon zest
2 ½ cups cake flour
2 ½ cups all-purpose flour
½ tsp. baking powder
½ tsp. salt

Icing:
4 cups confectioners sugar
⅓–½ cup boiling hot water
1 oz. bittersweet chocolate,
  chopped fine
1 tsp. light corn syrup

1. Preheat oven to 375°F.
2. Using a mixer fitted with a
   paddle attachment, cream sugar
   and butter together on medium
   speed until fluffy. Add eggs
   1 at a time, blending between
   additions. With the motor still
   running, add milk, vanilla, and
   lemon zest and blend well.

SPECIAL SUPPLIES

Electric mixer
Double boiler
**Spring-loaded
ice cream scoop**
Pastry brush
Baking sheets (2)
Parchment paper
Wire rack

3. Meanwhile, whisk the flours, baking powder, and salt together in a medium bowl. Add to the egg mixture and blend thoroughly.

4. Using a spring-loaded ice cream scoop, scoop out the dough and place each scoop 2 inches apart on baking sheets lined with parchment paper. Bake until the sides of the cookies begin to brown slightly, about 18 to 20 minutes.

5. Cool completely on a wire rack.

6. While the cookies are cooling, make the icing: Place confectioners sugar in a large mixing bowl. Gradually stir in boiling water until the sugar reaches a thick, spreadable consistency.

7. Pour half the frosting in the top half of a double boiler. Add the chocolate and corn syrup and set over simmering water. Warm the mixture, stirring, until the chocolate has melted and the frosting is smooth. Turn off the heat, but leave the chocolate frosting over the hot water to maintain its spreadable consistency.

8. Using a pastry brush, coat half of each cookie top with chocolate frosting, and the other half with white frosting. Let dry, and store in an airtight container.

Chocolate Peanut Butter Fudge

This delicious fudge marries rich chocolate with salty peanut butter.

Makes 4 pounds

28 oz. sweetened condensed milk
24 oz. bittersweet chocolate chips
¼ tsp. sea salt
24 oz. peanut butter chips

SPECIAL SUPPLIES

Saucepan
Baking pan
(9 by 13-inch)
Parchment paper
Aluminum foil
Plastic wrap

1. Line a 9 by 13-inch baking pan with a layer of foil, then place a layer of buttered parchment paper on top of the foil.
2. In a saucepan over medium heat, stir together 12 oz. condensed milk, bittersweet chocolate chips, and sea salt. Heat until chocolate chips are completely melted and smooth. Pour the mixture into the prepared baking pan and smooth out to the sides.
3. Heat the peanut butter chips and remaining condensed milk in a clean saucepan over medium heat until chips are completely melted and smooth. Spoon mixture carefully on top of chocolate mixture. Smooth to the sides of the pan.
4. Cover with plastic wrap and refrigerate until firm, about 45 minutes.
5. Remove the fudge from the pan and cut into squares. Store up to 2 weeks in an airtight container.

Churro Bites

It's well worth it to make these warm, cinnamony bites of heaven from scratch.

Makes 36 churro bites

1 cup water
½ cup unsalted butter, cut into pieces
¼ tsp. ground cinnamon
¼ tsp. salt
1 ½ cups all-purpose flour
3 large eggs
2 large egg whites
canola oil
¼ cup granulated sugar
1 tsp. ground cinnamon

SPECIAL SUPPLIES

Large saucepan
Medium saucepan
Candy/deep fry thermometer
Pastry bag
Paper towels

1. In a medium saucepan over medium heat, bring water, butter, cinnamon, and salt to a rolling boil. Add flour all at once, mixing with a wooden spoon to quickly incorporate. Cook, stirring constantly, until thickened, about 3 minutes.
2. Remove saucepan from heat and let stand to cool until steaming subsides, about 5 minutes. Add eggs and egg whites 1 at a time, beating thoroughly after each addition. Scoop batter into a pastry bag and set aside.
3. In a large saucepan, heat about 4 inches of canola oil over medium heat until the temperature registers 360°F. Carefully hold the pastry bag over the hot oil and squeeze out a strip of dough about 1 inch long. Snip off the dough strip with scissors and let it drop into the oil. Fry about a dozen bites at a time, turning once, until golden brown, about 1 minute each side.
4. Using a slotted spoon, transfer the bites to paper towels to absorb excess oil. Fry remaining churros, adjusting heat as necessary between batches to maintain oil temperature. Let the churros cool completely.
5. Meanwhile, combine sugar and cinnamon in a bowl. When the churros are cool, roll them in the sugar mixture to coat.

Funnel Cake with Berries

Funnel cake at the fair is as American as the Ferris wheel.

Makes 6 to 10 funnel cakes

6 tbsp. unsalted butter, cut into smaller pieces
1 cup cool water
½ tsp. sea salt
½ tsp. granulated sugar
1 ½ cups all-purpose flour
3 large eggs
2 large egg whites
canola oil
confectioners sugar

SPECIAL SUPPLIES
Electric mixer
Stockpot
Medium saucepan
Candy/deep fry thermometer
Pastry bag
Wire rack

1. Combine butter, water, salt, and sugar in a medium saucepan over medium-high heat. Bring to a boil over high heat. Remove from heat and quickly stir in the flour. Return the pan to low heat and cook, stirring frequently, for about 3 minutes to cook the flour slightly and rid the mixture of any starchy, floury taste.

2. Remove the pan from the heat and place the dough in the bowl of a mixer fitted with a paddle attachment. Mix on medium speed until most of the steam has subsided, then add the eggs and egg whites, one at a time, until each is incorporated and a batter is formed.

3. Pour 3 inches of oil into a stockpot and heat to a temperature of 350°F.

4. Meanwhile, place the batter in a pastry bag fitted with a round tip no wider than ¼ inch in diameter.

5. Holding the pastry bag over the hot oil, push the batter out into the hot oil in a zig-zag or spiral shape. Fry no more than 1 large or 2 smaller funnel cakes at a time.

6. Fry the cakes until puffed up and golden (they will triple in size), 3 to 5 minutes, flipping every 30 seconds or so.

7. Drain the cakes on a rack and cool slightly, then sprinkle with confectioners sugar and add the Berry Topping (recipe follows).

Berry Topping

1 qt. fresh berries, cleaned and sliced
½ cup granulated sugar
pinch sea salt

1. Combine berries, sugar, and salt in a bowl. Let stand for 30 minutes before serving.

Marbleized Chocolate Strawberries

A twist on the classic chocolate-covered strawberry.

SPECIAL SUPPLIES

**Double boiler
Baking sheet
Parchment
paper**

Makes 24 strawberries

24 long-stemmed strawberries, washed and dried
16 oz. bitter or semisweet chocolate
4 oz. white or milk chocolate

1. Place the berries in rows on a baking sheet lined with parchment paper. Refrigerate for at least 30 minutes prior to dipping.
2. To melt the chocolate, place in a bowl on top of a double boiler over medium heat, stirring until melted. To avoid burning the chocolate, heat the water to just rippling for the bitter/semisweet chocolate and just steam for the white/milk chocolate.
3. Pour the bitter/semisweet chocolate in a deep bowl. Using a spoon, drizzle about ⅓ of the white/milk chocolate onto the top surface of the darker chocolate.
4. Holding them by the stem, dip the strawberries into the chocolate. Do not swirl the berries—plunge them directly into the chocolate and then pull them back out. Both chocolates will adhere to each berry's surface.
5. Place the berries on parchment paper and allow the chocolate coating to harden. As you continue to dip the berries, drizzle more white/milk chocolate onto the surface of the bitter/semisweet chocolate as needed.

Chocolate-Encased Bacon

Most fair vendors serve this bacon frozen, since the chocolate melts fast in the heat of the day.

Makes 12 strips

12 strips applewood bacon
1 lb. chocolate candy coating
sea salt

SPECIAL SUPPLIES

Double boiler
Skewers
(twelve 10-inch)
Pastry brush
Baking sheets (2)
Parchment paper
Paper towels

1. Preheat oven to 400°F.
2. Thread bacon strips onto skewers and place on 2 baking sheets lined with parchment paper. Bake for 20 minutes, turning bacon strips halfway through.
3. Drain and pat excess oil away with paper towels. Meanwhile, melt chocolate coating in a bowl over a double boiler.
4. Using a pastry brush, coat bacon strips evenly with chocolate on both sides. Place strips on a clean baking sheet lined with parchment paper and sprinkle with sea salt. Let cool.
5. Refrigerate until ready to serve.

> Melt a second color of chocolate separately and drizzle over the coated bacon to decorate.

Chocolate Cupcakes with Fudge Frosting

These rich cupcakes have a double dose of chocolate and are iced with fudge frosting!

Makes 12 cupcakes

SPECIAL SUPPLIES

Electric mixer
Muffin pan (12-cup)
Paper muffin liners
Saucepan (2-quart)
Wire rack

Cupcakes:
1 ¼ cups all-purpose flour
½ cup cocoa powder
¾ tsp. baking soda
¼ tsp. sea salt
1 cup granulated sugar
⅓ cup canola oil
1 large egg
1 tsp. vanilla extract
¾ cup buttermilk
½ cup semisweet chocolate chips

Fudge Frosting:
¼ cup unsalted butter
4 oz. unsweetened chocolate, chopped fine
3 ½ cups confectioners sugar
½ cup whole milk

1. Preheat oven to 350°F.
2. In a bowl, whisk together flour, cocoa powder, soda, and salt. Set aside.
3. Using a mixer fitted with a paddle attachment, cream sugar, oil, egg, and vanilla. Add the flour mixture alternately with the buttermilk, making 3 additions of the flour mixture and 2 of the buttermilk. Stir in chocolate chips.
4. Scoop batter into a muffin pan lined with paper cupcake liners. Bake for 22 to 27 minutes, or until a toothpick inserted in the center comes out clean. Cool completely.
5. To make the frosting, heat butter and chocolate in a 2-quart saucepan until melted. Set aside.
6. Using the mixer fitted with a paddle attachment, combine confectioners sugar and milk. Slowly stir in the chocolate mixture until combined.
7. Remove the mixing bowl and refrigerate for 10 minutes. Place the bowl back in the mixer and beat with the paddle attachment until it reaches the desired whipped texture. Frost cupcakes liberally.

Texas Jumbo Chocolate Chunk Cookies

Everything at the Texas State Fair is jumbo-size! These cookies will soon become a family favorite.

2 cups minus 2 tbsp. cake flour
1 ⅔ cups bread flour
1 ¼ tsp. baking soda
1 ¼ tsp. baking powder
1 ½ tsp. sea salt
1 ¼ cups unsalted butter, room temperature
1 ¼ cups light brown sugar, packed
1 ¼ cups granulated sugar
2 large eggs
2 tsp. pure vanilla extract
1 ¼ lbs. semisweet chocolate (60%), chopped coarsely

SPECIAL SUPPLIES
Electric mixer
Spring-loaded
ice cream scoop
Baking sheets (2)
Parchment paper
Wire rack

1. Preheat oven to 350°F.
2. In a large bowl, whisk together cake flour, bread flour, baking soda, baking powder, and sea salt. Set aside.
3. Using a mixer fitted with a paddle attachment, cream butter and both sugars until light and airy. Add eggs 1 at a time, mixing well after each addition. Stir in the vanilla and chocolate chunks. Reduce speed to low and add flour mixture, blending until just combined, 5 to 10 seconds.
4. Using a spring-loaded ice cream scoop, place balls of dough onto baking sheets lined with parchment paper. Press down on the dough with the palm of your hand to flatten. Bake until golden brown but still soft, 18 to 20 minutes.
5. Transfer baking sheets to a wire rack for 10 minutes, then slip cookies onto another rack to cool a bit more.

Chocolate Marshmallows

Once you make your own marshmallows, you'll never buy the packaged kind again.

Yield: 1 ½ pounds

3 ½ envelopes unflavored gelatin
½ cup cold water
2 cups granulated sugar
½ cup light corn syrup
½ cup hot water (about 115°F)
¼ tsp. sea salt
2 large egg whites
1 tsp. pure vanilla extract
1 oz. unsweetened chocolate, melted and cooled
¾ cup confectioners sugar

SPECIAL SUPPLIES

Electric mixer
Heavy saucepan (3-quart)
Baking pan (9 by 13-inch)
Candy/deep fry thermometer

1. In a mixing bowl fitted with a whip attachment, sprinkle gelatin over cold water and let stand to soften.
2. Meanwhile, in a heavy, 3-quart saucepan over medium heat, cook granulated sugar, corn syrup, hot water, and salt, stirring with a wooden spoon until sugar is dissolved. Increase heat to medium and boil the mixture, without stirring, until a digital or candy thermometer registers 240°F, about 12 minutes.

3. Remove pan from heat and pour the sugar mixture over the gelatin in the mixing bowl. Mix on low speed until gelatin is dissolved, then beat on high speed until the mixture is white, thick, and nearly tripled in volume, about 6 minutes.

4. Clean the whip attachment, then beat egg whites in a large bowl just until they hold stiff peaks. Add the egg whites and vanilla to the sugar mixture and beat until just combined. Fold in unsweetened chocolate.

5. Spray a 9 by 13 by 2-inch baking pan with non-stick cooking spray and dust the sides and bottom with confectioners sugar. Pour marshmallow mixture into the pan and sift ¼ cup confectioners sugar evenly over the top. Refrigerate, uncovered, until firm, at least 3 hours and up to 1 day.

6. Run a thin knife around edges of the pan and invert onto a large cutting board. Lifting up 1 corner of the inverted pan, loosen the marshmallow with your fingers and let it drop onto the cutting board. With a large knife, trim edges of the marshmallow, then cut into roughly 1-inch cubes. Sift remaining confectioners sugar into a large bowl, then add marshmallows in batches, tossing to coat evenly.

7. Store in an airtight container at cool room temperature for up to 1 week.

Double Chocolate Cheesecake Brownies

These brownies layer creamy cheesecake over rich, luscious chocolate.

Makes 12 brownies

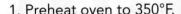

SPECIAL SUPPLIES

Electric mixer
Double boiler
Baking pan
(9 by 13-inch)

Chocolate Cheesecake Layer:

8 oz. cream cheese,
   room temperature
2 tbsp. unsalted butter,
   room temperature
½ cup granulated sugar
2 tbsp. Dutch process cocoa powder
1 tbsp. all-purpose flour
2 large eggs
2 tbsp. sour cream
1 tsp. pure vanilla extract

Brownie Layer:

½ cup unsalted butter, room
temperature
½ cup sugar
2 large eggs
8 oz. semisweet chocolate
1 tsp. pure vanilla extract
¼ tsp. salt
½ cup all-purpose flour

1. Preheat oven to 350°F.
2. First, make the chocolate cheesecake layer: Using a mixer fitted with a paddle attachment, blend cream cheese and butter on medium speed for about 2 minutes. Mix in sugar, cocoa powder, and flour. Add eggs 1 at a time, mixing after each addition, then mix in sour cream and vanilla. Scrape into a separate bowl and set aside.
3. After cleaning the mixing bowl fitted with the paddle attachment, make the brownie layer: In a double boiler over simmering water, melt chocolate completely and then remove from heat and allow to cool. Using the mixer, blend butter, sugar, and eggs on medium speed, then add chocolate, vanilla, and salt, mixing well. Turn off the mixer and, using a rubber spatula, fold in the flour just until blended.
4. Smooth the brownie mixture into the bottom of a 9 by 13-inch baking pan sprayed with non-stick cooking spray. Top with the chocolate cheesecake mixture, smoothing the batter out over the brownie mixture.
5. Bake until firm to the touch and dry-looking on top, about 25 to 30 minutes. Cool in the pan.

Four-Chocolate Brownies

A chocoholic's dream! Top these brownies with ice cream and prepare to be transported straight to heaven.

Makes 24 brownies

14 oz. unsweetened chocolate, chopped
¼ cup Dutch process cocoa powder
1 ½ cups unsalted butter, room temperature
3 cups granulated sugar
1 tsp. salt
6 large eggs
2 cups all-purpose flour
1 cup milk chocolate chips
1 cup semisweet chocolate chips

SPECIAL SUPPLIES
Electric mixer
Double boiler
Baking pan
(9 by 13-inch)
Wire rack

1. Preheat oven to 325°F.
2. In a double boiler, melt unsweetened chocolate with cocoa powder. Stir and set aside.
3. Using a mixer fitted with a paddle attachment, cream butter, sugar, and salt on medium speed for 2 minutes. Add eggs and mix for 4 minutes until fluffy. Add melted chocolate mixture, then add flour, mixing on a lower speed. Fold chocolate chips into batter.
4. Transfer to 9 by 13-inch baking dish lined with foil and sprayed with non-stick cooking spray. Bake in preheated oven until a toothpick inserted into the center comes out with loose crumbs and top is firm, about 35 to 40 minutes. Let cool on a wire rack before cutting into squares.

Circus Rainbow Cake
with Snowy White Buttercream Icing

This whimsical cake has layers in a rainbow of colors that children love!

Serves about 12

Cake:
4 ½ cups cake flour
1 tbsp. baking powder
½ tsp. sea salt
1 ¼ cups unsalted butter, room temperature
2 cups granulated sugar
6 large egg whites
2 tsp. pure vanilla extract
1 cup water, cold
3–6 drops each of red, orange, yellow, and green food paste coloring

Icing:
1 cup vegetable shortening
1 cup unsalted butter, room temperature
1 tsp. pure vanilla extract
1 lb. confectioners sugar
rainbow nonpareils

1. Preheat oven to 350°F.
2. In a large bowl, whisk together flour, baking powder, and salt. Set aside.

SPECIAL SUPPLIES

Electric mixer
Cake pans
(four 9-inch)
Cake circle (9-inch)
Parchment paper
Wire rack

3. Using a mixer fitted with a paddle attachment, cream butter and sugar until fluffy. With the mixer running, add egg whites 1 at a time, beating 1 minute between each addition.

4. In a pourable container, stir vanilla and water together and add to butter mixture alternately with flour mixture, beating until batter is smooth and well-blended.

5. Divide batter into 4 small bowls. Color each bowl of batter with a different food paste coloring.

6. Pour batter separately into four 9-inch cake pans, each sprayed with non-stick cooking spray and lined with parchment paper. Bake until a toothpick inserted into the cake comes out clean, about 18 to 22 minutes.

7. Cool cakes in their pans for 10 minutes. Remove cakes and place on a rack to cool completely.

8. Meanwhile, make the icing: Using a mixer fitted with a paddle attachment, blend shortening and butter until soft and fluffy. Add vanilla extract and about half of the confectioners sugar. Whip on slow speed until very soft and fluffy. Scrape the bowl down with a rubber spatula and whip for a few minutes longer on a higher speed. Add the remaining confectioners sugar and mix on slow speed until blended. Finally, set the mixer on medium speed and whip icing until very fluffy.

9. To decorate the cake: Once the cakes have cooled completely, place the green layer on a 9-inch cake circle. Spread about ¼ of the icing on top. Place the yellow layer on top of the green layer and, again, spread ¼ of the icing on top. Repeat with the orange layer, and then place the red layer on top. Spread the remaining icing over the entire exterior of the cake. Sprinkle with rainbow nonpareils.

Fruity Snow Cones

Experiment with different Kool-Aid® flavors to create your own unique snow cone syrups!

1 ½ cups granulated sugar
1 ½ cups water
Two 16-oz. packages Kool-Aid® unsweetened
  powdered drink mix
ice cubes

SPECIAL SUPPLIES
Food processor or snow cone maker
Medium saucepan

1. Bring sugar and water to a boil in a medium saucepan over medium heat. Turn off the heat, add Kool-Aid®, and stir. Let cool. Store in a sealed bottle or container.
2. Place ice cubes in food processor or snow cone maker. Process to make slushy ice.
3. Fill cones with ice. Pour syrup over ice and serve.

Frozen Cheesecake on a Stick

A fresh take on cheesecake—frozen, enrobed in chocolate, and served on a stick!

Makes 12 cheesecakes

Filling:
1 lb. cream cheese, room
 temperature
¾ cup granulated sugar
2 large eggs
2 tbsp. fresh lemon juice
½ tsp. pure vanilla extract
1 lb. chocolate candy coating

SPECIAL SUPPLIES

Electric mixer
Double boiler
Cheesecake pan
(10-inch)
Wooden dowels (12)
Baking sheet
Parchment paper
Plastic wrap
Wire rack

Crust:
⅓ pound graham crackers, crushed
¼ cup unsalted butter, melted

1. Preheat oven to 350°F.
2. Mix the graham crackers and butter in a bowl. Press into a cheesecake pan and freeze until firm, about 15 minutes.
3. Using a mixer fitted with a paddle attachment, mix cream cheese and sugar together, blending until creamy. Add eggs, 1 at a time, while mixing. Add lemon juice and vanilla and blend well.
4. Pour batter into the frozen cheesecake bottom, smoothing it out to touch the sides. Bake until the top starts to pull away from the sides and still look a bit loose in center, about 35 to 40 minutes. It will look like it is puffed up. Remove from the oven and set on a rack until cool to the touch.
5. Keep the cheesecake in the pan. Wrap with plastic wrap and refrigerate for 12 hours. Unmold cheesecake and cut into 12 slices. Rewrap in plastic wrap, and place in freezer for 1 hour.
6. Melt chocolate coating in a double boiler. Dip the wooden sticks into the chocolate, then insert each stick through the cheesecake slices horizontally, from the wide end to the pointed end. Place all pieces back into freezer for 10 minutes.
7. Dip each piece of frozen cheesecake into the candy coating and set on a baking sheet lined with parchment paper to dry. Serve immediately.

Gingerbread Man Cookies

Some county fairs are held later in the year and sell holiday cookies. These cookies are wintertime classics.

Makes 3 dozen cookies

1 ¾ cups all-purpose flour
½ tsp. baking soda
½ tsp. ground ginger
½ tsp. ground cinnamon
¼ tsp. sea salt
⅛ tsp. ground cloves
¼ cup unsalted butter
¼ cup brown sugar, packed
¼ cup molasses
5 ½ tbsp. cool water

SPECIAL SUPPLIES
Electric mixer
Gingerbread man
cookie cutters
(2½-inch)
Rolling pin
Baking sheets
Parchment
paper

1. Preheat oven to 375°F.
2. In a medium bowl, whisk together flour, baking soda, ginger, cinnamon, salt, and cloves. Set aside.
3. Using a mixer fitted with a paddle attachment, cream butter and sugar. Beat in molasses.
4. Add water and dry ingredients alternately to the butter mixture. The dough will become very stiff; you may have to mix the last dry ingredients by hand.
5. On a floured surface, work the dough like bread dough, kneading until smooth in consistency. Roll the dough out on a slightly floured surface to ¼ inch thick. Press a 2 ½-inch gingerbread man cookie cutter into the dough.
6. Place the gingerbread men on baking sheets lined with parchment paper. Bake until crisp, about 10 to 12 minutes.

Caramel Apples

Caramel apples are required eating at the fair. Here's how to make your own from scratch.

Makes 6 apples

6 large, tart apples, washed, with stems removed
¾ cup unsalted butter, room temperature
1 ½ cups brown sugar, packed
¾ cup light corn syrup
10 ½ oz. sweetened condensed milk
1 ½ tsp. pure vanilla extract
toppings of your choice (sprinkles, chopped nuts, etc.)

SPECIAL SUPPLIES

Large saucepan
Medium saucepan
Wooden dowels (6)
Candy/deep fry thermometer
Baking sheet
Parchment paper

1. Fill a large saucepan with water, about ¾ of the way to the top. Bring to a boil. Use a large slotted spoon to dip each apple into boiling water for a few seconds to remove any wax (if you skip this step, the caramel will not adhere to the apples).
2. Dry the apples thoroughly with a towel and refrigerate for 20 minutes to cool them down. When completely cold, insert wooden dowels into the apples.
3. Stir butter, brown sugar, and sweetened condensed milk in a medium saucepan over medium-high heat. Stirring constantly, bring the mixture to a boil, then reduce heat to medium. Still stirring, cook the mixture until a candy thermometer reads 248°F, about 25 to 30 minutes. Remove from heat and stir in vanilla extract.
4. Dip each apple into the hot caramel, tilting the pan to coat them completely. Set apples on a baking sheet lined with parchment paper and let sit for about 30 minutes. Before the caramel dries completely, add toppings to the coating, if desired.

Granny Smith and Pippin apples make delicious caramel apples.

Mini Spiced Apple Doughnuts

Most fair vendors have an automatic doughnut maker that produces dozens per minute. Here is a simple way to make your own doughnuts without a fryer.

Makes 12 mini doughnuts

SPECIAL SUPPLIES

Mini doughnut pan (12-well)
Pastry bag
Wire rack

Doughnuts:
2 ½ cups cake flour
1 cup granulated sugar
2 ½ tsp. baking powder
2 tsp. ground cinnamon
1 tsp. ground nutmeg
½ tsp. sea salt
¾ cup whole milk
½ cup canola oil
2 large eggs
1 tsp. pure vanilla extract
1 ½ cup finely chopped baking apples
½ cup chopped pecans (optional)

Topping:
⅓ cup granulated sugar
2 tsp. ground cinnamon
1 tsp. ground nutmeg
½ tsp. ground mace

1. Preheat oven to 325°F.
2. In a large bowl, whisk together cake flour, sugar, baking powder, cinnamon, nutmeg, and salt. Set aside.
3. In a medium bowl, whisk together milk, oil, eggs, and vanilla. Add to flour mixture, mixing only to blend. Fold in apples and pecans, if desired.
4. Place batter in a pastry bag and squeeze the batter out into the wells of a greased mini doughnut pan. Press the batter into each crevice of the pan, about ⅔ full.
5. Bake until each doughnut springs back when lightly touched, about 10 to 14 minutes. Let cool in the pan for 10 minutes, then pop the doughnuts out and cool completely on a cooling rack.
6. Meanwhile, make the topping: Blend sugar, cinnamon, nutmeg, and mace in a small bowl. Toss cooled doughnuts in the mixture to coat.

Rich Vanilla Bean Ice Cream

Vanilla is the most popular ice cream flavor in the country. If you have never used a real vanilla bean before, now is your chance!

Makes 1 quart

3 cups heavy cream
1 cup whole milk
¾ cup granulated sugar
2 whole vanilla beans, split,
  with the seeds extracted
4 large egg yolks

SPECIAL SUPPLIES

Ice cream
freezer
Saucepan

1. Heat the cream, milk, sugar, and vanilla beans in a saucepan over medium heat, stirring occasionally until the sugar is dissolved and the mixture is hot.
2. Whisk the egg yolks in a small bowl. Pour about 1 cup of the hot cream mixture over the eggs while whisking. Then take the egg mixture and pour into the heated cream. Cook over medium heat until the liquid coats the back of a spoon, about 8 minutes.
3. Strain the vanilla pods out of the mixture, then cool the liquid at room temperature for about 1 hour.
4. Place mixture into an ice cream freezer and freeze according to the manufacturer's instructions.

Snickerdoodle Cookies

This cinnamon sugar cookie has a slight puffiness to it, like a little cake.

Makes 3 dozen cookies

Dough:
3 ½ cups all-purpose flour
1 tbsp. baking powder
½ tsp. salt
2 cups granulated sugar
1 cup unsalted butter, room temperature
¼ cup heavy cream
2 large eggs

SPECIAL SUPPLIES
Electric mixer
Wire rack

Spice Topping:
¼ cup granulated sugar
2 tsp. ground cinnamon
2 tsp. freshly ground nutmeg

1. Preheat oven to 350°F.
2. In a large bowl, whisk together flour, baking powder, and salt. Set aside.
3. Using a mixer fitted with a paddle attachment, cream sugar and butter until fluffy. Mix in cream and eggs. Add flour mixture, blending only until well-combined.
4. Make the topping: Combine sugar, cinnamon, and nutmeg in a small bowl.
5. Scoop out walnut-size pieces of dough. Roll each ball of dough in the sugar mixture to coat. Place on cookie sheets lined with parchment paper and, using the palm of your hands, press down on dough to flatten a bit.
6. Bake until the cookies are light brown on the sides, about 10 to 12 minutes. Let sit on the baking sheets to cool, then move to a rack to cool completely.

Southern-Style Pecan Coffee Cake

This rich, moist cinnamon breakfast cake will enlighten your morning coffee. It can also be served as a light dessert.

Serves 12

1 ¼ cup pecans, chopped
3 cups plus 2 tsp. granulated sugar
3 tsp. ground cinnamon
1 ½ unsalted butter, room temperature
8 oz. cream cheese, room temperature
1 tbsp. fresh lemon juice
2 tsp. pure vanilla extract
6 large eggs
2 ⅔ cups cake flour
⅛ tsp. salt

SPECIAL SUPPLIES

**Electric mixer
Tube pan
(10-cup)
Wire rack**

1. Preheat oven to 350°F.
2. Mix ½ cup pecans, 2 tsp. sugar, and 1 tsp. cinnamon in a small bowl. Sprinkle mixture in the bottom of a 10-cup tube pan sprayed with non-stick cooking spray. Set aside.
3. Using a mixer fitted with a paddle attachment, cream remaining sugar, butter, and cream cheese on medium speed until fluffy, about 4 minutes. Add lemon juice and vanilla, mixing until well-blended. Add each egg 1 at a time, thoroughly blending into the batter, about 2 minutes for each egg.
4. Combine cake flour, remaining cinnamon, and salt in a large bowl. Add to egg mixture, mixing until well-blended, about 3 minutes. Remove the bowl from the mixer and fold remaining pecans into the batter, mixing with a spoon until combined.
5. Pour batter into the tube pan, smoothing to the sides. Bake until a toothpick inserted in the center comes out clean, about 1 hour and 20 minutes.
6. Leave cake in the pan to cool for 10 minutes, then turn upside down onto a cooling rack. Cool completely before cutting.

Lemon Mist Bars

These rich cookie bars are wonderful served with tea or lemonade.

Makes 36 bars

2 cups all-purpose flour
½ cup macadamia nuts, crushed and toasted
½ cup granulated sugar
1 cup unsalted butter, softened
2 tbsp. lemon zest
4 large eggs, beaten
2 cups granulated sugar
3 tbsp. all-purpose flour
½ tsp. baking powder
¼ cup fresh lemon juice

SPECIAL SUPPLIES
Baking pan
(9 by 13-inch)
Parchment
paper

1. Preheat oven to 350°F.
2. In a large mixing bowl, combine flour, half of the macadamia nuts, and sugar. Add the butter and half of the lemon zest, and mix together until well-combined.
3. Pat dough into the bottom of a 9 by 13-inch baking pan lined with parchment paper. Bake until golden brown, about 22 minutes.
4. Meanwhile, combine eggs, sugar, flour, baking powder, lemon juice, and the remaining lemon zest in a mixing bowl. Blend until well-combined.
5. Pour lemon mixture on top of the baked macadamia crust while still hot. Place pan back in the oven and bake for 20 minutes.
6. Sprinkle with confectioners sugar and the remaining macadamia nuts. Cut into bars while still warm. Allow to cool before serving.

The World's Gooiest Cinnamon Rolls with Cream Cheese Frosting

The best cinnamon rolls on the planet by far!

Makes 36 large cinnamon rolls

8 cups all-purpose flour
1 tsp. sea salt
2 tbsp. plus ½ tsp. ground cinnamon
1 ¼ tsp. ground nutmeg
½ cup warm water (about 110°F)
2 tbsp. rapid rise yeast
2 tbsp. granulated sugar
One 4-serving box instant vanilla
    pudding (Jell-O® brand preferred)
2 cups whole milk
½ cup unsalted butter, melted
2 large eggs, beaten
1 ½ cups brown sugar, packed
¼ cup unsalted butter, melted
½ cup toasted, chopped pecans
    (optional)

1. In a large bowl, whisk together flour, salt, ½ tsp. cinnamon, and ¼ tsp. nutmeg. Set aside.
2. In a small bowl, whisk together warm water, yeast, and sugar to dissolve. Let sit until foaming, about 5 minutes.
3. Using a mixer fitted with a paddle attachment, stir together pudding, milk, butter, and eggs just to blend. Place yeast mixture and 6 cups of flour mixture on top of the liquid mixture. Let sit for 5 minutes.
4. Turn the mixer on low and blend until the mixture starts to bind together. Switch to a higher speed, adding remaining flour and mixing until the sides of the bowl are clean.

156

5. Knead dough on a floured surface for 2 minutes, then place in a very large, greased bowl. Cover and let rise in a warm, non-drafty area for 40 minutes.
6. Meanwhile, in a small bowl, combine the brown sugar with the remaining cinnamon and nutmeg. Set aside.
7. Preheat oven to 375°F. Punch down the dough, then roll on floured surface to about 36 by 18 inches. Brush the melted butter on top. Sprinkle with the cinnamon mixture, leaving about 1 inch uncovered at the base.
8. Roll the dough up into a log, then cut into 1-inch sections, creating 36 cinnamon rolls.
9. Place rolls on a baking sheet lined with parchment paper, in 4 rows of 9 rolls. Bake until light brown, about 22 to 24 minutes.
10. Spread Cream Cheese Frosting (recipe follows) on rolls immediately after taking them out of the oven. Sprinkle with pecans, if desired. Serve hot.

Cream Cheese Frosting

Makes 3 cups (enough for 1 batch of cinnamon rolls)

8 oz. cream cheese, room temperature
½ cup unsalted butter, room temperature
1 tsp. pure vanilla extract
½ tsp. pure almond extract
3 cups confectioners sugar
3 tbsp. whole milk

1. Using a mixer fitted with a paddle attachment, blend cream cheese and butter on medium speed until softened. Add vanilla and almond extracts, then add confectioners sugar and blend on a higher speed to create a fluffier texture. Add milk in small increments until the frosting reaches a smooth, spreadable consistency.

Candy Apples

This classic fair staple is fun to make at home.

Makes 6 to 8 apples

6–8 medium apples, washed, with stems removed
3 cups granulated sugar
½ cup light corn syrup
1 cup cold water
3 drops red paste food coloring
2 tsp. pure vanilla extract

SPECIAL SUPPLIES

Large saucepan
Apple sticks (6–8)
Candy/deep fry thermometer
Pastry brush
Baking sheet
Parchment paper

1. Press an apple stick into each apple and set aside.
2. In a large saucepan, combine sugar, corn syrup, water, and food coloring. If any sugar granules end up on the inside of the pan, use a wet pastry brush to clean them down. Set the mixture over medium to high heat and bring to a boil. Insert a candy thermometer into the liquid and allow it to boil, without stirring, until it reaches 302°F (hard crack stage), about 20 minutes. Remove from heat.
3. Add vanilla and stir only slightly to blend. Working with 1 at a time, dip the apples into the mixture, tilting the pan to coat them evenly. Let the excess drip off into the pan, then set the coated apples on a baking sheet lined with parchment paper. Allow to dry for 30 minutes before eating.
4. Store covered in a cool, dry place. Do not refrigerate, or the candy coating will become soft.

Rome apples make the best-looking candy apples.

PHOTO CREDITS

Note: All appropriate lengths were taken to secure proper photo credits and permissions. Any omissions or errors are deeply regretted and will be rectified upon reprint.

Taryn Adams: 127

Sarah Almaskeen: 36

Tonya Becerra / Caraluna Studio: 13

Genevieve Bell: 16, 42

Christina Bello: 39, 106–107, 124–125, 152

Pier Francesca Casadio: 31, 120, 143, 155

Steven Depolo: 111

Ed Gately: 72

Tim Ebbs: 144–145

Dave Fimbres, SemiCharmedLifePhotography LLC: 26

Lisa Ghenne: 34–35

Rita Haverty, www.RitaBakez.com: 137

Brian Henrich (1977–2012), contributed in loving memory: 114

iStock.com/aizram18: 69

iStock.com/amberleeknight: 60

iStock.com/bhofack2: back cover (left), 41, 64–65

iStock.com/FtLaudGirl: 102

iStock.com/gontabunta: 80–81

iStock.com/jatrax: 25

iStock.com/Lecic: 20

iStock.com/margouillatphotos: 74–75

iStock.com/Nadore: 24

iStock.com/NoirChocolate: 88

iStock.com/nschatzi: back cover (upper right), 15

iStock.com/pilipphoto: 12

iStock.com/zirconicusso: 29

iStock.com/Vitalina: 21

iStock.com/Zoryanchik: 132

kaiskynet/Shutterstock.com: 140–141

Catherine Keeter: 76, 100–101

Mary Ann Lacy: 146

Mike Lang, AnotherPintPlease.com: 49, 98

L.A. County Fair: front cover (center, upper left, upper right, lower right), back cover (lower right), back cover and throughout (camel photo), 4, 5 (all), 6 (all), 7 (all), 8, 10–11, 27, 32–33, 50, 59, 62–63, 66, 79, 82, 85, 90–91, 93, 94–95, 112–113, 122–123, 134–135, 156–157

Evan Mackay: 22

Deena Mehta: 28, 45, 118–119

Michaela B Photography: 128

Anne Murphy: 56

Nuria Ocaña: 54–55

Bobby Pathammavong: 53

Craig Phillips: 97

Edward Sargent: 17

Jacqueline Sinclair: 23

Danica Skeoch: 130–131

Pauline Smith: 30

Bill Spoonster/Spoonster Photography: 117

Kylie Tefft: 158

David Thompson: 19

Judy Ulrick: 150–151

Diana Yang: front cover (lower left), 46–47, 104

ACKNOWLEDGMENTS

Technically, I grew up at the Los Angeles County Fairgrounds. When I was a child, my parents would take us to the fair every fall. I thank them both for the many hours we spent walking the midway and exploring the large buildings of exhibits. Now, when I'm traveling and a county or state fair is going on, I can't resist dropping in to compare it with my home fair.

I graduated from being a culinary judge to the culinary coordinator of the Los Angeles County Fair. In those twenty-eight years, I had the best judges—over 130 of them—for all the contests. Too many to name, but I thank you all. Thank you to Cyndi Harles of the Blue Ribbon Group and Beth Somers, formerly of Wilton Enterprises.

To my family and friends: Thank you to Neil for allowing me to drag you to all the fairs for the past thirty-five years. To Mom and Dad for being my biggest, most supportive fans. To Monica and Pattie for being great sisters. To Jonathan for being anywhere anytime at a moment's notice and a true friend.

Thank you to my last food crew at the Los Angeles County Fair: Val, Annette, Josephine, and Teri. You all worked countless hours to make dreams come true for the contestants.

To Renee Hernandez Diepenbrock of Fairplex Media, thank you for the countless hours of research and visuals. Thank you to Trina Kaye for being the best publicist ever.

In my seven years as the resident segment chef at CW6's *San Diego Living*, we had a great run. Thank you to the greatest segment producer, Tiffany Frowiss; to all the news anchors over the years, Marc Bailey, Heather Myers, Chase Cain, Lynda Martin, and Clint August; and to the "weather gals," Kim Evans and Renee Kohn. Thank you to all the floor managers— Jacob, Brent, Juan, and Jonah—for making me and my food look good.

Lastly, I want to thank the team at Santa Monica Press: Jeffrey Goldman for his insight on this project; Kate Murray for keeping my voice in the editing process and being a true delight to work with; and Amy Inouye for making this book so beautiful. This is my second book with this very talented team and I hope for many more.